Funkschau
Telecom

Funkschau
Telecom

Günter Glass

Fachbegriffe der Telekommunikation

Deutsch/Englisch – Englisch/Deutsch

6500 Begriffe, Umschreibungen und Fachwortbegriffe

Franzis'

Die Deutsche Bibliothek – CIP-Einheitsaufnahme

Glass, Günter:
Fachbegriffe der Telekommunikation : deutsch/englisch - englisch/deutsch ; 6500 Begriffe, Umschreibungen und Fachwortbegriffe / Günter Glass. -
München : Franzis, 1992
  (Funkschau : Telecom)
  ISBN 3-7723-4591-3
NE: HST

© 1992 Franzis-Verlag GmbH & Co. KG, München

Sämtliche Rechte - besonders das Übersetzungsrecht - an Text und Bildern vorbehalten. Fotomechanische Vervielfältigungen nur mit Genehmigung des Verlages. Jeder Nachdruck, auch auszugsweise und jede Wiedergabe der Abbildungen, auch in verändertem Zustand, sind verboten.

Satz: typo spezial Ingrid Geithner, Erding
Druck: Offsetdruck Heinzelmann, München
Printed in Germany - Imprimé en Allemagne.

ISBN 3-7723-4591-3

Vorwort

Telekommunikation gibt es seit langem. In jüngster Zeit hat dieser Bereich insbesondere durch die mobile Kommunikation gewaltigen Aufschwung erfahren. Dies schlägt auch in der Terminologie zu Buche.
Diese Fachbegriff-Sammlung versucht, die Standardbegriffe der heutigen Telekommunikation und die zahlreichen Fachbegriffe des Mobilfunks zu erfassen.
Der deutsch-englische Teil enthält ca. 3.000, der englisch-deutsche Teil ca. 3.500 Stichwörter.

Stuttgart, im April 1992

Deutsch-Englisch

A

abarbeiten (Befehle mpl)	to execute
(Rufe mpl)	to answer
(Unterbrechungen fpl)	to service
abbauen (Verbindung f)	to clear (a connection)
abbrechen (Protokoll n)	to disconnect
(Programm n)	to terminate, to abort
(Verbindung f)	to clear down
Abbruch m	disconnection, clear-down
Abfallzeit f (Impuls m)	pulse decay time, pulse fall time
abfangen	to lock out
Abflachschaltung f	smoothing circuit
Abfrage f	inquiry, polling
abfragebereit (Wahlcode m)	presented
Abfrage | gerechtigkeit f	first-come, first-served principle
~ modus m	inquiry mode
abfragen	to inquire, to interrogate, to answer
Abfrage | prüfimpuls m	interrogation test pulse
~ schaltung f	answering circuit
~ taste f	"who are you" key
~ - und Mitlesemaschine f	answering and monitoring machine
abgehend	outgoing, outbound, mobile-originated, mobile-to-land, mobile-to-base
abgesetzt (Endgerät n)	remote
abgestrahlte Leistung f	radiated power
Abgleich m	tuning

abgleichen	to line up, to compensate
abheben, abnehmen (Hörer m)	to lift, to take off (handset), to go off-hook
Abhörsicherheit f	security against tapping, safety from interception
Ablauf m	
teilnehmerbezogener ~	user-related sequence
vermittlungstechnischer ~	switching-oriented operation, call-processing sequence
ablaufen (Zeitgeber m)	to time out
Ablauf- und Refresh-Steuerung f	sequence and refresh control
Abmeldeanforderung f	log-off request, sign-off request
abmelden	to sign off, to log off
Abmeldung f	deactivation, log-off, sign-off
~santrag m	deactivation request
abnehmen, abheben (Hörer m)	to lift, to take off (handset), to go off-hook,
Abnehmer m, Abnehmer | leitung f	serving trunk, serving line
~ adresse f	serving port address
~ bündel n	serving trunk group
~ kanal m	serving channel
~ leitung f, gemeinsame ~	common serving trunk
Abreißen der Funkverbindung f	loss of radio contact
Abruf m	call(ing), recall(ing), polling, retrieval
~ en/Kopieren n aus dem Speicher m	retrieve/copy from memory
~ impuls m	call pulse
~ zeichen n	proceed-to-send signal
abschalten (Gerät n)	to switch off
(Lautsprecher m)	to mute
(MS)	to deactivate, to switch off
(Verbindung f)	to disconnect
Abschattung f	shadowing
abschnittweise übertragen	to transmit section by section
Absender m (einer Nachricht f)	originator

Abstand m zwischen Funkzonen fpl (gleicher Frequenz)	distance ratio, D/R
absteigend (Verkehr m)	descending
~ er Weg	descending path
Abstimmungszeichen n	handshaking signal
abstrahlen (Leistung f)	to radiate (power)
absuchen	to hunt
Absuchreihenfolge f	hunting sequence
abtasten (Signale npl, Impulse mpl)	to sample, to scan
Abtast | geschwindigkeit f	scanning speed
~ theorem n	sampling theorem
~ ung f	sampling, scanning
~ verzerrung f	sampling distortion
~ wert m	sample
zurückgebildeter ~ wert	reconstructed sample
~ zeitpunkt m	sampling instant
~ zeitraster n	sampling time-slot pattern
Abwärts | frequenz f	downlink frequency
~ strecke f (Verbindung f von BS zu MS; Strecke f vom Satelliten m zur Erdfunkstelle f)	downlink, downpath
Abweissignal n	non-acceptance signal
abwickeln (Verkehr m) (Verbindungen fpl)	to handle (traffic), to serve (calls)
Abwicklungszeit f	serving time
Abzweigstelle f	branch, branch-off point
Achternetz n, Doppelkreisnetz f	figure-of-eight network
adaptive Sendeleistungsregelung f	adpative transmitter power control
Ader f (Kabel n)	core, wire
(Lichtwellenleiterkabel n)	fiber
Adressenaufruf m	address call
A/D-Wandler m	analog-to-digital converter, analog-digital converter, A-D converter

Aktiv | datei f	check-in file, active subscribers file
~ - | Reserve-Betriebsart f	working/standby mode, on-line/standby mode
aktualisieren	to update
Aktualitätenspeicher m	current status memory
Akustikkoppler m	acoustic coupler
Akzeptanz f	acceptance
Alarm m	alarm
~ behandlung f	alarm handling, alarm processing
~ bei Trägerausfall m	carrier failure alarm
~ - und Notrufdienste mpl	alarm and emergency services
~ unterbrechungsanforderung f	alarm interrupt request
~ zustandsüberwachung f	alarm condition monitoring
dringender ~	major alarm
Alpha-Betriebsweise f (ISDN)	alpha mode
Amateurfunker m	radio amateur
Amplituden | modulation f, AM	amplitude modulation, AM
~ umtastung f	amplitude shift keying, ASK
~ verzerrung f	amplitude distortion
AMPS (amerikanisches Mobilfunksystem n)	AMPS (Advanced Mobile Phone System)
Amt n	exchange
bemanntes ~	attended exchange, manned exchange
übergeordnetes ~	higher-ranking exchange
unbemanntes ~	unattended exchange, unmanned exchange
amtsintern	cross-office
Amts | leitung f	exchange line
~ wählton m	exchange dial tone
~ zeichen n	start-dialling signal, proceed-to-send signal
Analog | -Digital-Wandlung f	analog-to-digital conversion A-D conversion, ADC
~ netz	analog network
~ telefon n	analog telephone

anbieten (Dienste mpl)	to provide
(Signal n)	to present
(Vermittlung f)	to offer
(Versorgung f)	to provide coverage
Anbieter m (Dienste mpl)	provider, service provider
(Gesprächszeit f)	airtime reseller
Anfangszeichen n	start-of-text character, STX character
Anforderung f der Gebührenübernahme	reverse charging request
~ der Standortinformation f	location information request procedure
~ssperre f, zentrale ~	central request lockout
Angebot n (Dienste mpl)	provision
(Signale npl)	presentation
(Verkehr m)	offered traffic
angemietete Übertragungswege mpl	leased lines
angeschlossen	on-line
Anklopfen n	call waiting
~ mit Anzeige f	call waiting with call number indication
akustisches ~	acoustic call waiting indication, acoustic camp-on
optisches ~	optical call waiting indication, visual camp-on
ankommend	incoming, inbound, mobile-terminated, land-to-mobile, base-to-mobile, terminating
Anlaufphase f	start-up phase
Anmeldeanforderung f	log-on request, sign-on request
anmelden	to log on, to sign on, to check in, to book (a call), to activate
Anmeldung f	activation, log-on, notification
Annahme f der Gebührenübernahme f	reverse charging acceptance
Anpassung f	matching, adaptation
Anreiz m	event
~ aus der Peripherie f	peripheral event
~verarbeitung f	event processing
ankommender ~	incoming event
gegenteiliger ~	conflicting event

gesicherter ~	verified event
interner ~	internal event
wartender ~	suspended event
Anruf m	call
abgehender ~	outgoing call, mobile-originated call
abgebrochener ~	dropped call, abandoned call
blockierter ~	blocked call
eingehender ~ , ankommender ~	incoming call, mobile-terminated call
erfolgloser ~	unsuccessful call, ineffective call
erfolgreich abgewickelter ~	successful call
fehlgeleiteter ~	misdirected call
gebührenfreier ~	no-charge call
gebührenpflichtiger ~	chargeable call, revenue call
selektiver ~	selective call
unangemeldeter ~	cold call
zustandegekommener ~	completed call
~ entgegennehmen	to answer a call
~ zwischen Mobilfunkteilnehmern mpl	mobile-to-mobile calls
Anruf | absicht f, **Verbindungswunsch** m, **Bedienungswunsch** m	call intent
~ annahme f	call acceptance
~ beantworter m	telephone answering set, answerphone
anrufen	to call, to ring (up), to phone, to make a call
Anrufer m	caller, calling party
bevorrechtigter ~	priority caller
Anruf | gerät n, **automatisches** ~	automatic call maker
~ häufigkeit f	call density
~ liste f	incoming call log
~ melder m	pager
~ schutz m	station forced busy, station guarding
~ signal n	calling signal
~ überführung f	"follow me"
~ übernahme f	call pickup
~ umleitung f	call diversion
~ umleitung f im Besetztfall m	call forwarding on mobile subscriber busy

~ umleitung f bei Nichterreichbarkeit f   call forwarding on mobile subscriber not reachable
~ verarbeitung f   call processing
~ versuch m   call attempt
~ verteiler m, automatischer ~   automated call distributor
~ verteilung f   mobile access hunting
~ wartefunktion f   camp-on function
~ warteschleife f   call hold
~ weiterleitung f   call forwarding
    bedingungslose ~ weiterleitung f   call forwarding unconditional
~ weiterleitung f bei belegtem Funkanschluß m   call forwarding on mobile subscriber busy, CFMSB
~ weiterleitung f bei Funküberlastung f   call forwarding on radio congestion, CFRC
~ weiterleitung f bei nicht gemeldetem Funkteilnehmer m   call forwarding on mobile subscriber not registered, CFMSNR
~ weiterleitung f wenn keine Antwort f   call forwarding on no reply, CFNR
~ weiterleitung f wenn keine Antwort f auf Meldeanruf m   call forwarding on no paging response, CFNPR
~ weiterschaltung f   handoff, call transfer
    automatische ~ weiterschaltung f   call forwarding on no reply
~ wiederholung f   reattempt

Ansage f   announcement
~ dienst m   recorded announcement service

anschalten, sich ~   to access

anschließen   to connect, to link, to interface

Anschluß | bereich m der Vermittlungsstelle f   exchange area
~ faser f (Lichtwellenleiter m)   pigtail
~ gebühr f   activation charge
~ gruppe f   line group, trunk group
gerufene ~ kennung f   called line identification, CLI
rufende ~ kennung f   calling line identification, CLI
~ leitung f   access line, link

anstehen   to wait to be served (service request), to wait to be answered (call), to wait to be attended (subscriber)

ansteuern   to activate, to select, to drive

Anstiegszeit f (Impuls)	ramp time
Anteil m zustandegekommener Verbindungen fpl	call completion rate
Antenne f	antenna, aerial
~ mit hohem Gewinn	high gain antenna
eingefahrene ~	retracted antenna
Empfangs ~	receiving antenna
isotrope ~	isotropic antenna
nach unten neigende ~	down-tilting antenna
oben beschwerte ~	top-loaded antenna
rundstrahlende ~	omni-directional antenna
umlegbare ~	tiltable antenna
Antennen | ausleuchtungsgebiet n	antenna coverage, antenna area
~ ausrichtung f	antenna orientation
~ diversity	antenna diversity
~ gewinn m	antenna gain
wirksame ~ höhe f	effective antenna height
~ koppler m	antenna multiplexer
~ kuppel f	radome
~ mast m	antenna mast
freitragender ~ mast m	self-supporting mast
~ mastaufbau m	mast erection
~ mastfundament n	mast foundation
~ mehrfachausnutzung f	antenna multiplexing
~ richtung f	antenna bearing
~ schaltdiversity	antenna switched diversity
~ standort m	antenna site, antenna location
~ turm m	antenna tower
antiparallelgeschaltet	back-to-back connected
Antwort | kennzeichen n ,,Zugang m verhindert''	access barred signal
~ ton m	answering tone
anwählen, wählen	to dial, to select
Anwendersoftware f, vermittlungstechnische ~	switching user software
Anwendungs | protokoll n (ISDN)	application protocol
~ schicht f	application layer
Anwesenheitszeichen n	presence signal

Anzapfen	wire tapping
Anzeige f der gerufenen Nummer f	connected number identification presentation, ConNIP
~ der gerufenen Nummer f gesperrt	connected number identification restriction, ConNIR
~ der rufenden Nummer f	calling number identification presentation, CNIP
~ der rufenden Nummer f gesperrt	calling number identification restriction, CNIR
~ der Nummer f des gerufenen Teilnehmers m	connected line identification presentation
~ der Nummer f des rufenden Teilnehmers m	calling line identification presentation
Anzeigefeld n für Dienstsignale npl	display panel for service signals
Anzeigenbedienung f	display handling
Apparat m, am ~ bleiben	to hold the line
Arbeitsmodus m	operating mode
Architekturmodell n	architecture model
Armbanduhr-Funkrufempfänger m	wrist-watch pager
ASCII (American Standard Code for Information Interchange)	ASCII (genormter Code für Nachrichtenaustausch)
Asynchron | betrieb m	asynchronous mode
~-/Synchron-Umsetzer m	asynchronous/sychronous converter
Audiokonferenz f	audioconference, telephone conference
Aufbau m, Aufforderung f zum ~ einer Verbindung f	connection request
aufbauen (Verbindung f)	to establish, to set up (connection, call)
Aufbauzeit f (einer Verbindung f)	connection setup time
Aufenthalts | bereich m	location area, LA
~datei f	location register
~funkzone f	visited radio zone
Aufforderungsphase f (zum Senden) (zum Empfangen)	inquiry phase polling phase
Auffrischalarm m	refresh alarm
aufgelegt, eingehängt	on-hook

auflegen	to go on-hook, to replace (receiver)
auflösen (Verbindung f)	to clear (a connection)
aufrufen (Prozedur f)	to invoke
Aufschaltemeldung f	trunk offering message
Aufsuchen n der Standortinformationen fpl	location information retrieval procedure
aufsteigend (Verkehr m)	ascending
Aufwärts	frequenz f	uplink frequency
~ strecke f (Verbindung f von MS zu BS; Strecke f von der Erdfunkstelle f zum Satelliten m)	uplink
Aufzeichnung f	recording
~ mit Gleichstromvormagnetisierung f	DC bias recording
~ mit Rückkehr f nach Null	return-to-zero recording
~ mit Rückkehr f zum Bezugszustand m	return-to-reference recording
~ ohne Rückkehr f zum Bezugszustand m	non-return-to-reference recording
Ausbau	gebiet n	expansion area
~ stufe f	configuration level
Ausbreitung f (Wellen fpl/Licht n)	propagation
ausbreitungsbedingte Frequenzmodulation f	random frequency modulation
Ausbreitungs	dämpfung f	loss relative to free space
~ geschwindigkeit f	propagation rate, speed of propagation
~ messungen fpl	propagation measurements
~ modell n	propagation model
~ verlust m	propagation loss
~ verzögerung f	propagation delay
~ vorhersage f	propagation forecast, propagation prediction
~ weg m	propagation path
ausbuchen	to log out
Ausdehnung f, räumliche ~ eines Netzes n	coverage of a network, distance covered by a network, distance to be covered by a network

Ausfall m	failure, outage
~ abstand m, mittlerer ~	mean time between failures, MTBF
~ rate f	failure rate
ausfallsicher	fail-safe
nicht ~	non-failsafe
Ausfallwahrscheinlichkeit f	probability of failure
Ausgangs | punkt m	output port
~ stellung f	home position
~ zeitlage f	outgoing time slot
ausgeben (Meldungen fpl)	to send (messages)
ausgehängt, abgenommen	off-hook
Aushängeanreiz m	off-hook event
Auskunfts | dienst m	information service
~ dienste mpl	directory inquiry services, inquiry services, information services
Auslands | fernmeldedienst m	external telecommunications
~ fernwahl f	international DDD
~ vermittlung f	international gateway exchange, international gateway center
Auslastungsgrad m	usage factor
Ausleuchtung f (Antenne f)	illumination
ausrufen, jemanden ~	to page
Ausrichtfehler m (Antenne f)	pointing error
Außendienst m	field service
Aussendungen fpl, unerwünschte ~	unwanted emissions
Außerband | -Emission f	out-of-band emission
| -Signalisierung f, ~ -Zeichengabe f	out-band signalling
Austast | lücke f	blanking interval
~ signal n	blanking signal
austauschen (Daten)	to exchange
~ , ersetzen	to replace (A by B), to substitute (B for A)
(gegenseitig) ~	to interchange

Ausweich | bündel n — alternate trunk group
~ leitweg m — alternate route
auswerten (Dienstsignale npl) — to analyze (service signals)
Auto | korrelationsfunktion f, AKF — autocorrelation function
~ -Münzfernsprecher m — drive-in coin telephone
autorisieren — to authenticate
Auto | -Telefaxgerät n — roadfax
~ telefon n — mobile telephone, car telephone, carphone, vehicular mobile radio unit
~ telefondienst — automobile telephone service
~ telefon-Teilnehmer m — automobile telephone subscriber

B

Backbone-Netz n (zur Verbindung f inkompatibler Netze npl) — backbone network
Ballungsgebiet n (Gewerbe n und Industrie f) — area of industrial concentration
Bändertausch m, Bandumsetzung f — frequency frogging
Band | breite f — bandwidth
~ filter n — bandfilter, bandpass filter
~ invertierung f — band inversion
~ paß m — bandpass
~ umsetzung f, Bändertausch — frequency frogging
Basis | anschluß m (Netz n) — basic access
~ anschluß-Multiplexer m — basic interface multiplexer
~ band n — baseband
~ bandfrequenz f — baseband frequency
~ bandgerät n — baseband equipment
~ dienstmerkmal n — basic service attribute
~ kanal m — basic access, B channel

~prozessor m	base processor
~station f, Funkfeststation f, ortsfeste Landfunkstelle f	base station, BS
betreuende ~station f, versorgende ~station f	serving base station
transportable ~station f	portable cell site
~stationsbereich m, Bereich m einer Funktfeststation f, Funkverkehrsbereich m	base station area
~stationsschnittstelle f	base station interface, BSI
~stationssteuerung f	base station controller, BSC
Baud, Bd	baud, bd
Baudot-Code m (Fernschreiber m)	Baudot code (five-channel code)
Baumstruktur f	tree structure
BCH-Code	BCH (Bose-Chauduri-Hocquenghem) code
Bearer Services, Trägerdienste mpl (bei ISDN)	bearer services
Bedarfs | prüfung f	demand test
~zuteilung f	demand assignment
Bedeckung f, Versorgung f	coverage
Bedeckungsgrad m, Versorgungsgrad m	degree of coverage
bedienbare Teilnehmerzahl f	customer handling capacity
bedienen	to serve (subscribers)
Bediener | anfrage f	operator inquiry
~führung f	prompts, prompting, operator guidance
akustische ~führung	voice prompting
~oberfläche f	operating surface
bedienter Betrieb m	attended operation, manned operation
Bedien- und Anzeigefeld n	control and display panel
Bedienungs | bereich m	service area
~wunsch m, Verbindungswunsch m, Anrufabsicht f	call intent
Befehlsvorrat m	instruction set, instruction repertoire
erweiterter ~	extended instruction set, extended instruction repertoire

beheben (Fehler m)	to recover, to correct (an error), to remedy (a defect)
beidseitige Übertragung f	two-way transmission, both-way transmission
Belastungsteilung f, Teilung f der Verkehrslast f	call load sharing
belegen (Leitung f)	to seize (a line)
belegt	busy, seized, occupied
Belegtzustand m	busy condition
Belegung f	occupancy, seizure
abgewiesene ~	lost call
angebotene ~	offered call
angenommene ~	carried call
erfolgreiche ~	successful call
gehende ~	outgoing seizure
kommende ~	incoming seizure
verzögerte ~	delayed call
wartende ~	waiting call
Belegungs | abstand m	inter-arrival time (of calls)
mittlerer ~ abstand m	mean time between seizures
~ befehl m	seizure command
mittlere ~ dauer f	mean holding time
~ muster n	call pattern
~ versuch m	line seizure attempt, attempt to occupy mobile stations
Messung f der Anzahl f der ~ versuche mpl	peg count
~ versuche mpl während der Hauptverkehrsstunde f	busy hour call attempts, BHCA
~ zeit f	occupancy time, busy time, holding time
~ zusammenstoß m	head-on collision, call collision
~ zustand m	busy state, occupance, occupance state
benachbart (z.B. Kanal m)	adjacent, neighbouring
benachbarte Basisstation f	neighbouring base station
~ Funkzone f	adjacent radio zone
benutzbar, nicht ~, nicht zugänglich	accessible, inaccessible
Benutzer m (s.a. Teilnehmer m)	user
benutzerfreundlich adj	user-friendly

Benutzer | freundlichkeit f — user friendliness
~ gruppe f — user group
  geschlossene ~ gruppe f — closed user group
~ klasse f — user class of service, class of service
~ -Netz-Signalisierung f — user-network signalling
~ schnittstelle f — user interface
~ teil m (ISDN) — user part

Berechtigung f — connection privilege, authorization
  personenbezogene ~ — personal authorization

Berechtigungs | karte f — access card
~ klasse f — class of service
~ zeichen n — right-of-access code

Bereichskennzahl f — area code

Bereitschafts | betrieb m — hot standby
~ dienst m — standby service

Bereitstellung f — activation process, provision
~ stellungsgebühr f, — non-recurring activation charge
  einmalige ~ stellungsgebühr f
~ stellungsgebühr f pro Verbindung f — establishing charge
~ zustand m — ready condition, ready state

Beruhigungston m, Musikein-
  spielung f im Haltestand m — music-on-hold

beseitigen (Fehler m) — to eliminate, to correct,
to remove (a fault)

Besetzt | anzeige f — busy indication
~ anzeigeterminal n — busy display terminal
~ lampenfeld n — station busy display panel
~ ton m — busy tone
~ zeichen n — busy signal
  akustisches ~ zeichen n — audible busy signal
~ zustand m — busy state

Bestellterminal n — teleshopping terminal

Besucherdatei f — visitor location register, VLR,
visitor file, roamers' file

Besuchsschaltung f — follow-me transfer

besuchte Funkvermittlungsstelle f — visited mobile services switching
center, visited MSC, visited exchange

~ Mobilfunknetz n	visited public land mobile network
~ Netz	visited network
Betreiber m	operator, carrier
~ gesellschaft f, Betriebsgesellschaft f	operating company
betreuen, versorgen	to serve
Betrieb m, außer ~	out of service
~ ~ (Sender m)	off the air
in ~	in service, in operation
~ ~ (Sender m)	on the air
privilegierter ~	privileged operation
Betriebs | art f	mode of operation, operating mode
~ artenwechsel m	mode change
~ bereich m	service area, coverage area
betriebsbereit	ready-to-operate, operational
Betriebs | bereitschaft f überprüfen	to exchange status information
~ daten f	in-service data
~ güte f	quality of service, grade of service
~ sperrsignal n	operations inhibit signal
~ system n für Datenfernübertragung f	communications operating system
~ technik f	operation and maintenance
betriebstechnische Organisation f	adminstration and maintenance organization
Betriebs- | und Datenserver m	administration and data server
~ - und Wartungszentrum n	operations and maintenance center, OMC
~ wechsel m	mode change
~ weise f	mode of operation, operating mode
~ zulassung f	operating licence
~ zustand m	power-up mode
~ zustandsanzeige f	status indication
Beugung f	diffraction
Beugungs | dämpfung f, Beugungsschwund m	diffraction loss
~ modell n	diffraction model
Bevorrechtigung f	priority
bevorrechtigter Anrufer m	priority caller

beweglich, ortsveränderbar, mobil	mobile
bewegliche Funkstelle f, Mobilstation f, MS	mobile station, MS
~ Landfunk m	land mobile radio
~ Landfunkdienst m	land mobile radio service
~ Landfunkstelle f	land mobile station
Bewegtbild | kommunikation f	full-motion video communications
~ -Telekonferenz f	full video teleconference, videoconference
bewerten	to analyze, to weight
Bezugs | frequenz f	reference frequency
~ takt m	reference clock pulse
bidirektional adj	bidirectional
biegbarer Hohlleiter m	semirigid waveguide
BIGFON (breitbandiges integriertes Glasfaser-Fernmelde-Ortsnetz n)	wideband optical fiber local communications network
Bild | fernsprechen n	videophoning, video-telephony
~ fernsprecher m	videophone, video display telephone
~ kommunikation f	video communications, image communications
~ konferenz f	videophone conference
~ schirmpost f	screenmail
~ schirmtelefon n	video telephone, video display telephone
~ schirmtext m („Btx"), Videotex (internationale Bezeichnung)	videotex
Breitband-~ schirmtext m	broadband videotex
~ signalübertragung f	video signal transmission
Billigtarif m	off-peak rate
Bit | ausblendung f	bit suppression
~ bündel n	bit burst
~ bündelübertragung f	burst transmission
~ fehlerrate f, ~ fehlerhäufigkeit f	bit error rate
~ fehlerwahrscheinlichkeit f	bit error probability
~ rate f	bit rate
~ synchronisation f	bit synchronization
bit-transparent	bit transparent

Bit | übertragungsprotokoll n	physical protocol
~ übertragungsschicht f	physical layer
B-Kanal m (Nutz- oder Basiskanal m im ISDN)	B channel, basic channel
Blindbelegung f	blind occupation
Block | code m	block code
~ fehlerhäufigkeit f, ~ fehlerrate f	block error rate
~ fehlerwahrscheinlichkeit f	block error probability
Blockierung f	blocking
äußere ~	all trunks busy
innere ~	internal blocking
Blockierungsdauer f	all-trunks-busy time
blockierungsfrei	non-blocking
Blockierungswahrscheinlichkeit f	blocking probability
blockorientierte Zugangsprozedur f	block-oriented access procedure
Blockprüfzeichenfolge f	frame checking sequence, FCS
Boden | funkstelle f	ground radio station
~ station f, Erdfunkstelle f	earth station
Brechung f (Lichtwellenleiter)	refraction
Brechungs | gesetz n	Snell's law
~ koeffizient m	refractive index, index of refraction
Brechzahlprofil n	refractive index profile
Breitband-Bus m	broadband bus
Breitband | dienst m	broadband service, wideband service
~ fernmeldenetz n, integriertes ~ fernmeldenetz n	integrated broadband communications network
breitbandiges integriertes Glasfaser-Fernmeldenetz n, BIGFERN	wideband integrated fiber optical long-distance communications network
~ ~ ~-Ortsnetz n, BIGFON	wideband integrated optical fiber local communications network
Breitband/-ISDN (B-ISDN)	broadband ISDN
~ kanal m	broadband channel
~ kommunikation f	wideband ~, broadband communications

~ koppelfeld n	broadband switching network
~ teilnehmeranschluß m	broadband user line
~ übertragung f	broadband transmission, wideband transmission
~ -Vermittlungstechnik f	broadband switching
~ -Wähldienst m	dialled broadband (wideband) service
Bridge (Verbindung f zwischen gleichartigen lokalen Netzen npl)	bridge
Briefkasten m, elektronischer ~	electronic mailbox
Brummen n	hum
Brummunterdrückung f	hum suppression
Btx-Zentrale f	videotex computer center
Bündel n	trunk group, line group
~ fehler m	burst error
~ funk m	trunking
~ spaltung f, ~ trennung f	trunk group splitting
Bürokommunikation f	office communications
Burstübertragung f	burst transmission
Bus m	bus
~ netz n	bus-type network
~ struktur f	bus structure, bus architecture
~ topologie f	bus topology
~ zuteiler m	bus arbiter
Byte n	byte

C

CCIR (Comité Consultatif International des Radiocommunications) (International Radio Consultative Committee) — internationaler beratender Ausschuß m für den Funkdienst m)

CCITT (Comité Consultatif International Télégraphique et Téléphonique) (International Telegraph and Telephone Consultative Committee) — internationaler beratender Ausschuß m für den Telegrafen- und Fernsprechverkehr m

CCITT-Empfehlung f — CCITT standard

CEPT (Conférence Européenne des Administrations des Postes et Télécommunications) (European Conference of Postal and Telecommunicationa Administrations) — Europäischer Zusammenschluß m der Post- und Fernmeldeverwaltungen fpl

Chipkarte f — chip card, smart card

Chipkarten | -Fernsprecher m — chip-card telephone
~ leser m — smart card reader, chip card reader

Cluster n, Funkzonengruppe f, Zellbündel n — cluster
~ maß n, ~ größe f, ~ zahl f — cluster size
~ -Steuerung f — cluster controller

C-Netz n (450-MHz-Bereich) — C network

Code m der Zielvermittlungsstelle f — destination point code

Code m, fehlerkorrigierender ~ — error correcting code

codetransparent	code-transparent (independent of code structure)
Computerpost f	comail
Container m	utility trailer
~ -Vermittlungsstelle f	container installation
CSMA/CD (carrier sense multiple access with collision detection)	Vielfach-Zugriffsverfahren n mit Kollisionserkennung f
C-Verstärker m	class-C amplifier

D

D1-Netz n (900-MHz-Bereich)	D1 network, D1 system
D2-Netz n (900-MHz-Bereich)	D2 network, D2 system
D1-Betreibergesellschaft f	D1 operator
D2-Betreibergesellschaft f	D2 operator
Dachantenne f	roof-top antenna
dämpfen (z.B. Signal n)	to attenuate
Dämpfung f, Leistungsabfall m, Leistungsverlust m (in dB)	attenuation (dB), loss
Darstellungs | protokoll n	presentation protocol
~ schicht f	presentation layer
Dateiserver m	file server
Dateldienst m (der Bundespost f)	Datel service (data telecommunications)
Daten | abfragesignal n	polling signal
einleitender ~ austausch m	handshake
~ dienste mpl	data services
~ einleitungszeichen n	message prefix signal
~ endeinrichtungen fpl, DEE	data terminal equipment, DTE
~ endgerät n	terminal

~ fernschaltbaugruppe f	data communications equipment
~ festnetz n	dedicated circuit data network
~ funk m	radio data transmission
~ kanal m	data channel, information channel
gemeinsamer ~ kanal	centralized data channel
~ multiplexer m	data multiplexer
eigenständiges ~ netz	dedicated data network
~ netzkennzahl f	data network identification code, DNIC
~ paket n	packet
~ paketvermittlung f	packet switching
~ quelle f (Sendestelle f)	data source
~ rate f	bit rate
~ satz m	data record, record
~ schutz m	data protection
~ schutz m	privacy of personal data
~ senke f (Empfangsstelle f)	data sink
~ sicherheit f	data security
~ sicherung f	backing up
~ sicherungsschicht f, Verbindungsschicht f	link layer
~ station f (Datenendeinrichtung f + Datenübertragungseinrichtung f)	terminal station
~ teilnehmer m	data terminal subscriber
~ übermittlungsdienste mpl	data transmission services
~ übermittlungsnetz n	data communication network
~ übertragungseinrichtung f, DÜE	data circuit equipment, DCE, data circuit terminating equipment, data communications equipment
~ übertragungsvorrechner m	front-end processor
~ umschaltesignal n	data escape signal
~ verbundleitung f	computer PABX circuit
~ wählverkehr m	switched data traffic
~ weiche f	data selector
Datex/-Dienst m (der Bundespost n)	datex service (data exchange)
~ -L-Netz (Datex-Leitungsvermittlungsnetz n)	datex line switching network
~ netz-Abschlußgerät n	datex network termination unit
~ -P-Netz (Datex-Paketvermittlungsnetz n)	datex packet switching network
Daueranforderung f	continuous request

Dauer f der unnötigen Belegungen fpl	line lockout time
Dauer | empfangszustand m	continuous receive state
~ mäander m	continuous 400 µs timing signal
~ zyklusanforderung f	continuous cycle request
D/A-Wandler m	digital-to-analog converter, digital-analog ocnverter, D-A converter
Decodierungsfreigabe f	enable decoding
Deemphasis, Nachentzerrung f	de-emphasis
Dekadenwahl f	decade selection
dekomprimieren	to decompress
Deltamodulation f	delta modulation, DM
Demodulation f	demodulation
Demodulator m	demodulator
Demultiplexer m	demultiplexer
Depaketierung f	packet disassembly
Deregulierung f (Fernmeldemonopol m)	deregulation
Dezibel n, dB	decibel, dB
Diagnosepaket n	diagnostic packet
Dialog m mit Quittierung f	acknowledged interaction
~ betrieb m	dialog mode
~ steuerung f	dialog control
Dienst | art f	service category
~ attribut n	service attribute
~ bereich m, Netzbereich m	service area
Dienste mpl	services
erweiterte ~	enhanced services
höhere ~	higher-level services
Mehrwert ~	value-added services
Dienste | anbieter m, Dienstebringer m (Wiederverkäufer m von Gesprächszeit f)	service provider airtime reseller
~ angebot n	service provision
Diensterweiterung f	service enhancement

Diensteintegration f	service integration
diensteintegrierendes digitales Netz n	integrated services digital network, ISDN
Dienste | spektrum n	service mix
~ versorgung f	service coverage
~ wechsel m	change of service
Dienst | güte f	grade of service, service quality
~ leistungsmerkmal n	service feature
~ merkmal n	service attribute; (ISDN) facility
~ signal n	service signal
~ teilnehmer m	service user
~ übergang m	service interworking
dienstüberschreitende Kommunikation f	interservice communication
Dienstverkehr m	service traffic
differentielle Phasensprungmodulation f, Phasendifferenzumtastung f	differential phase shift keying, DPSK
Differenz-Puls-Code-Modulation f	differential pulse code modulation, DPCM
diffuse Reflexion f	diffuse reflection
Diffusionsmodell n	diffusion model
digitaler Kurzwellenfunk m	digital short-range radio, DSRR
digitale Schnittstelle f für die Anbindung f von Basisstationen fpl	digital interface for radio control
digitalisieren, digital darstellen	to digitize
Digital | knoten m	digital node
~ netz n	digital network
~ signalverbindung f	digital link, digital path
~ technik f	digital technology
digital übertragen	to transmit digitally
Digitalvermittlungsstelle f	digital exchange
Dipolantenne f	dipole antenna
Direktbündel n	primary trunk group, first-choice trunk group

direkt durchgeschaltete Verbindung f	direct station-to-station connection
Direkt | ruf n	direct call
~ rufeinrichtung f	direct call facility
~ rufnetz n	leased-circuit data network
öffentliches ~ rufnetz n	public leased-circuit data network
direktstrahlender Satellit m	direct broadcasting satellite
Direkt | wahl f	direct dialling
~ weg m	primary route, first-choice route, direct route
~ zugriffkanal m	random access channel, RACH
Diversity f	diversity
Diversity | -Empfang m, Mehrfachempfang m	diversity reception
~ -Empfänger m	diversity receiver
~ -Gewinn m	diversity gain
D-Kanal m (Steuerkanal m im ISDN)	D channel
D-Kanal-Protokoll n	D channel protocol
Doppel | belegung f	double seizure
~ brechung f (Lichtwellenleiter m)	double refraction
~ kreisnetz n, Achternetz n	figure-of-eight network
~ stromtastung f	double-current keying
Doppler | -Frequenz f	Doppler frequency
~ -Leistungsspektrum n	Doppler power spectrum
~ -Verbreiterung f	Doppler spread
drahtgebundene Übertragung f	wire connection, line connection
drahtlos	wireless
~ es Datennetzwerk n	local area wireless network, LAWN
Drahtnetz n	wireline network
DRCS (frei programmierbarer Zeichensatz m)	DRCS (dynamically redefinable character set)
Dreierkonferenz f	three-party conference
Drei | -Teilnehmer-Dienste mpl	three-party services, TPS
~ -Teilnehmer-Gespräch n	three-party service
Dringlichkeitskennzeichen n	precedence signal
drücken (Taste f)	to press, to depress, to operate, to actuate

Duplex, Gegensprechen n	duplex, full duplex
~abstand m	duplex spacing
~kanal m	duplex channel
~übertragung f	full-duplex transmission
~verbindung f, ~fähige Verbindung f	duplex circuit
Durchgang m, auf ~ prüfen	to test for continuity
Durchgangs | fernleitung f	gateway
~knoten m	transit node
~verbindung f	transit call
~verkehr m	transit traffic
~vermittlungsstelle f	tandem, tandem switching center, transit switching center, transit exchange
internationale ~vermittlungsstelle f	international transit exchange
durchgeschaltet	through-connected
Durchsage f	voice message
Durchsatz m	throughput
~klasse f	throughput class
Durchschalte | betrieb m	line switching
~leistung f	call throughput rate
~vermittlung f	line switching, circuit switching
Durchschaltung f	through-connection
Durchwahl f	direct inward dialling, DID, direct dialling-in, DDI, direct outward dialling
mit ~ bis zur Nebenstelle f	with direct inward dialling (DID) to the extension
~nummer f	direct-dialling number
Dynamikbereich m	dynamic range
dynamische Kanalzuteilung f	dynamic channel assignment

E

EBCDIC-Code m (8-Bit-Code)	EBCDIC (extended binary-coded decimal interchange code)
Echo n	echo
unerwünschtes störendes ~	objectionable echo
Echo | betrieb m	echoplexing, echoplex transmission
~ kanal m	echo channel
~ kompensationsverfahren n	echo compensation method
~ kompensator m	echo canceller
~ prüfung f	echo check
~ unterdrückung f	echo compensation
Eigen | nachführung f	autotracking
~ test-Software f	self-test software
~ verzerrung f	inherent distortion
Ein | -/Ausgabe-Codewandler m	input-output code converter
~ -/Ausgabe-Prozedur f	input-output procedure
Einbrecheralarm m	burglar alarm
einbuchen	to sign on, to check in, to log in, to log on, to register
Einbuchen n in die Standortdatei f	location registration
Einbuchungsauftrag m	check-in request
Einfall m, streifender ~	grazing incidence
Einfügungsdämpfung f	insertion loss
Eingabeberechtigung f	input authorization
Eingangs-Kopfvermittlungsstelle f	terminating international exchange
Eingangs | koppler m	input matrix
~ rauschen n	front-end noise

eingehängt, aufgelegt	on-hook
einleitender Datenaustausch m	handshake
Einmodenfaser f, Monomodefaser f	single-mode fiber
einprägen (Spannung f)	to impress (voltage)
einschalten (Mobilstation f)	to activate (mobile station)
Einschaltspitze f	startup peak
Einseitenband-Amplitudenmodulation f	single sideband amplitude modulation
einseitig gerichtet	one-way . . .
Einstiegs-MSC, Eingangs-MSC	gateway mobile services switching center (MSC), gateway MSC, gate MSC
Einstrahlung f	irradiation
Einwegbetrieb m, Simplexbetrieb m	simplex mode, one-way mode
Einzel | abrufbetrieb m	single character call forward mode
~ abtastimpuls m	discrete sampling pulse
~ berechnung f	detailed billing, itemized billing
~ gesprächsnachweis m	individual call verification
~ kanal-Durchschaltung f	single-channel through-connection
Einzellenpuffer m	one-cell buffer
Einzeltakt m	single clock pulse
Einzugsbereich m (der Basisstation f)	base station area
elektromagnetische Verträglichkeit f	electromagnetic compatibility
elektronische Post f	electronic mail
~ Postfach n	electronic mailbox
~ Telefonbuch n	electronic telephone directory
Empfänger m	receiver
Empfänger | antenne f	receiver antenna
~ schwellwert m	receiver threshold
~ seite f	receiving end
Empfang m	reception
automatischer ~	unattended reception (facsimile)
Empfangs | antenne f	receiving antenna
~ auswerter m	interpreter circuit
empfangsbereit	ready to receive, receive ready

Empfangs | bereitschaft f	ready-to-receive state
~ bestätigung f	reception confirmation signal, receipt confirmation
~ betrieb m	receive mode
~ funkstelle f, ortsfeste ~ funkstelle f	receiving land station
~ güte f	reception quality
~ pause f	receive pause
~ puffer m	receive buffer
~ qualität f	reception quality
~ quittung f	receive acknowledgement
Emulationsservice m	emulation service
emulieren	to emulate
End | amt n	local exchange
~ benutzer m	end user
~ einrichtung f für den zentralen Zeichengabekanal m	signalling link terminal
~ einrichtungen fpl	terminal equipment
~ gerät n	terminal
~ geräte npl	terminal equipment
~ stellenrechner m	terminal computer
~ vermittlungsstelle f	local exchange
E-Netz n (1,8-GHz-Bereich)	E network
Entfernungs | messung f, relative ~	relative distance measurement
~ zone f	distance zone
Entkoppler m	decoupler
Entnahme f von Rückinformationen fpl	extraction of upstream information
entstören	to suppress interference, to clear faults
Entstörung f	interference suppression, fault clearance
entweichen (Signale npl)	to escape
Entzerrer m	equalizer
Entzerrung f, adaptive ~	adaptive equalization
envelopeweise Übertragung f	envelope-mode transmission

Enveloppe, Envelope
  (Bitgruppe f zu übertragender Daten, ergänzt durch 1 Zustands- und 1 Synchronisierbit n)
envelope

Erdfunkstelle f
~ funksystem n
earth station
terrestrial radio system

erdgebunden
ground-based

ereignisgesteuert
event-driven

Erinnerungssignal n
reminder signal

Erlang n, Erl (Einheit f des Verkehrswertes m einer Leitung f) (0 Erl = dauernd frei (1 Erl = dauernd belegt)
Erlang, Erl (traffic unit)

Erlangsche Verlustformel f
Erlang's loss formula

Erreichbarkeit f
  begrenzte ~
  konstante ~
  volle ~
availability
limited availability
constant availability
full availability

Ersatz | anlage f
~ kanal m
~ leitung f
~ weg m
back-up system
standby channel, alternative channel
fall-back circuit
alternate route

Erst | ausbau m (Amt n)
initial capacity, initially-installed capacity

~ inbetriebnahme f
~ weg m
initial startup
primary route, first-choice route

erweiterungsfähig
upgradable, expandable

Ethernet
Ethernet (LAN = local area network of Digital, Intel and Xerox)

europäischer Funkrufdienst m, Euro-Signal n
European radio paging system

Europakarte f
Eurocard (European standard size printed circuit board)

Europa-Münzer m
European coin telephone

europaweit
pan-European

europaweiter Funkrufdienst m — European radio messaging system, ERMES

europaweite GSM-Standards mpl — pan-European GSM standards

Euro-Signal n (Europäischer Funkrufdienst m) — European radio paging service

Externumschaltung f — intercell handoff, interhandoff

Extrembelegung f — extreme traffic load

F

fadingfrei — fading-free

Faksimile n (s. Fernkopieren) — facsimile

falschgeleitet, fehlgeleitet — misrouted, missent

falsch verbunden — wrong number

Faltungscodierung f — convolutional coding

Fangdaten fpl — malicious call identification data, malicious call tracing data

Fangen n — call tracing, malicious call identification

Farbfernkopieren n — colour telefax

Faser | dämpfung f (Lichtwellenleiter m) — fiber attenuation, fiber loss

~ hülle f — fiber buffer

~ mantel m — fibre cladding

~ optik f — fibre optics

FDMA-Zugriffsverfahren n — frequency division multiplex access

Fehlausrichtung f (Antenne f) — mispointing

Fehler m — fault, error, bug, defect

~ beheben — to correct, to remedy (a fault)

~ beseitigen (Software) | to debug
~ beseitigen | to remove, to eliminate, to clear (a fault)
  vorübergehender ~ | transient error
  wieder auftretender ~ | recurring error
  wiederholt auftretender ~ | repetitive error

Fehler | benachrichtigung f — notification of transmission errors
~ erkennung f — fault detection, error detection
~ erkennungscode m — error detecting code
~ erscheinungsbild n — pattern of faults
~ häufigkeit f — error rate

fehlerkorrigierender Code m — error correcting code

Fehler | schutz m, Fehlersicherung f — error protection
~ wahrscheinlichkeit f — error probability

Feintakt m — fine-time clock pulse

Feld | eichung f — field calibration
~ stärke f — field strength
~ stärkepegel m — signal level
~ verteilung f, diskrete ~ (Lichtwellenleiter mpl) — discrete field distribution

Fern | ablesen n (von Zählern m) — remote reading (of meters)
~ amt n — long-distance exchange, trunk exchange, toll exchange
~ diagnose f — remote diagnosis
~ gespräch n — long-distance call
~ kopie f, Faksimile n übertragen — to transmit a facsimile

fernkopieren — to facsimile, to telecopy

Fern | kopierer m — facsimile unit
~ laden n — downloading
~ leitung f — trunk line, long-distance line
  alle ~ leitungen fpl besetzt — all trunks busy, ATB
~ leitungsnetz n — trunk network
~ meldeamt n — telecommunications office
~ meldeanlagen fpl — telecommunications equipment, telecommunications installations
~ meldebetriebsgesellschaft f — carrier, carrier company
~ meldedienste mpl — telecommunications services
~ meldegeheimnis n — privacy of telecommunications, secrecy of telecommunications

~ meldegesellschaft f — telecommunications operator
öffentliche ~ meldegesellschaft f — public telephone operator
private ~ meldegesellschaft — private telephone operator
~ melde-Infrastruktur f — telecommunications infrastructure
~ meldenetz n — telecommunications network
~ meldesatellit m — communications satellite

europäisches ~ meldesatellitensystem n — European Communications Satellite System, ECS

~ meldeturm m — radio tower
~ meldeweg m, Übertragungsweg m — transmission path
~ messen n — telemetering, telemetry
~ münzer m — DDD coinbox telephone
~ nebensprechen n — far-end crosstalk
~ netz n — trunk network, long-distance network
~ schreib-Code m, 5-Bit-~ schreib-Code m — five-level telegraph code
~ schreiber m — teletype, teleprinter
~ schreib- und Datennetz n — telex and data network
öffentliches ~ sprechamt n — public telephone exchange
~ sprechansagedienst m — public recorded information service
~ sprechapparat m mit Tastenwahl f — pushbutton set
~ sprechauftragsdienst m — absent subscriber service
~ sprechauskunft f — directory assistance, directory inquiries (service)

analoges ~ sprechnetz n — analog telephone network
digitales ~ sprechnetz n — digital telephone network
öffentliches ~ sprechnetz — public switched telephone network, PSTN

privates ~ sprechnetz — private telephone network
~ sprechwählnetz n — dial-up telephone network, switched telephone network

~ verbindungsleitung f — trunk line
~ vermittlung f — trunk exchange, toll center, long-distance switching center, long-distance exchange

~ wahl f — direct distance dialling, DDD; subscriber trunk dialling, STD

~ wirkanlage f — telecontrol plant

~wirken n	telecontrol
~wirknetz n	telecontrol network
~wirktechnik f	remote control technology
~wirkverbindung f	telecontrol link
Festbild | kommunikation f	still picture communication, freeze-frame communication, fixed-image communication
~-Telefonkonferenz f	fixed-image teleconference
festgeschaltet	dedicated, non-switched
Festkörperkoppler m	solid-state matrix
festlegen, zeitlich	to time
Festnetz n	landline network, fixed network, land telephone network
~teilnehmer m	landline subscriber
~verbindung f	permanent circuit connection
Festverbindung f,	
internationale ~	international permanent circuit connection
terrestrische ~	terrestrial permanent circuit connection
flächendeckendes Netz n	full-coverage network
Flächen | deckung f	coverage
~kleinzone f	omni cell
~kleinzonennetz n	omnidirectional system
~modell n	area-to-area model
~nutzung f	land usage
Flugzeugtelefon n (öffentlicher Telefonanschluß m im Flugzeug n)	airfone
(Telefonapparat m pro Sitzreihe f)	seatphone
(Telefonservice m für Flugpassagiere mpl von British Telecom)	skyphone
Fluktuationsrate f	turnover, attrition rate (of customers/subscribers)
Folge | gebühr f	overtime rate
~signal n	successor signal
Freigabe | signal n	enable signal
~liste f (für Kanäle mpl)	free-channels table

Frei | raumausbreitung f	free space propagation
~ raumdämpfung f	free space basic transmission loss, free space attentuation
freischalten, freigeben	to release, to enable
Frei | sprechapparat m	hands-free telephone
~ sprechen n	hands-free operation, hands-free talking
~ ton m	ringing tone
~ wahl f	hunting
~ zeichen n	start of ringing, call-connected signal, ringback signal
~ zeichenquittung f	ringback acknowledgement
Fremd | bereich m	visited mobile services switching center area, visited MSC area
~ datei f	visitor location register, VLR
frequenzabhängig	frequency-sensitive
Frequenz | band n	frequency band
~ bereich m	frequency range
~ codemodulation f	frequency code modulation, FCM
~ diversity	frequency diversity
Frequenzen fpl verteilen	to allot frequencies
~ zuteilen	to assign frequencies
~ zuweisen	to allocate frequencies
frequenzgefiltert	frequency-selective
frequenzgeteilt	frequency-division . . .
Frequenz | hub m	frequency swing, frequency shift
~ hub m (Daten fpl)	data deviation
~ hub m (Sprache f)	speech deviation
~ kanalbündel n	radio channel group, frequency group
frequenzkonstant	frequency-stabilized
Frequenz | korrelationsfunktion f	frequency correlation function
~ modulation f, FM	frequency modulation
ausbreitungsbedingte ~ modulation f, stochastische ~ modulation f	random frequency modulation
~ multiplexer m	frequency multiplexer
~ multiplexbündelung f	frequency-division multiplex grouping
~ multiplexverbindung f	frequency-division multiplex connection

~ multiplexverfahren n	frequency-division multiplexing, FDM
~ ökonomie f	spectrum efficiency, spectral efficiency, frequency economy
frequenzselektiver Schwund m	frequency-selective fading
Frequenz | spektrum n	frequency spectrum, radio frequency spectrum
~ sprungverfahren n	frequency hopping
~ stabilität	frequency stability
~ umtastung f	frequency shift keying, FSK
~ verteilung f (an Länder npl, Gebiete npl)	frequency allotment
~ weiche f	frequency separating filter
~ wiederbenutzung f	frequency reuse, channel reuse
~ wiederbenutzungsfaktor m	frequency reuse factor
~ wiederholung f	frequency reuse
~ zuteilung f (an Funkstellen fpl, Teilnehmer mpl)	frequency assignment
~ zuweisung f (an Dienste mpl)	frequency allocation
Fresnelzone f	Fresnel zone
FSK-Träger m	audio tone frequency shift modulated carrier
FTZ (Fernmeldetechnisches Zentralamt n)	federal bureau for telecommunications
Fünfercode m (Fernschreiben)	five-level code
Funk | bereichskennzahl f	area code
~ dienst m	radio service
~ empfänger m	radio receiver
~ empfang m	radio reception
~ feld n	radio link hop
~ felddämpfung f	radio wave damping, system loss
~ feldlänge f	hop length
~ fernsprechdienst m	mobile radio telephone service
~ fernsprechen n, Sprechfunk m	radiotelephony
~ fernsprechnetz n	radiotelephone network
zellulares ~ fernsprechsystem n	cellular radiotelephone system
~ fernsteuerung f	radio control
~ feststation f, Basis-	base station

station f, ortsfeste Land ~ stelle f
betreuende ~ feststation f serving base station
~ frequenz f radio frequency
~ horizont m radio horizon
~ kanal m radio channel
~ netz n radio network
  zellulares ~ netz n cellular radio network
~ netzentwurf m radio network design
~ netzkennzahl f service code, service access code
~ ortungsdienst m radio location service
~ ortungsnetz n radio location network
~ peilfahrzeug n radio detector van
~ ruf m paging, radio paging
~ ruf m mit Textanzeige f display paging
~ ruf m beantworten to answer a page
~ rufbereich m calling area
~ rufdienst m radio paging service
  alphanumerischer ~ rufdienst m alphanumeric paging
  Europäischer ~ rufdienst m European radio paging service
  (Euro-Signal n)
  europaweiter ~ rufdienst m European radio messaging system, ERMES
~ rufdienst mit optischer Anzeige f display paging
~ rufempfänger m pager
~ rufendgerät n paging terminal
  europaweites ~ rufsystem n pan-European paging
  öffentliches ~ rufsystem n off-site paging
  privates ~ rufsystem n on-site paging
~ rufsender m radio transmitter
~ signal n radio signal
~ sprechdienst m mobile telephone service
  bewegliche ~ stelle, Mobilstation f mobile station
~ stille f auferlegen to impose silence
~ störgrad m radio interference level
~ störspannung f radio noise voltage
~ störung f radio interference
~ teilnehmer m radio subscriber
  vom ~ teilnehmer m abgehend mobile-originated
  beim ~ teilnehmer ankommend mobile-terminated
~ telefon n mobile phone, mobile telephone, radiotelephone

~ telefondienst m | radiotelephone service
Mobil ~ telefonnummer f, | mobile subscriber number
~ teilnehmernummer f

Funktionsteilung f | function sharing

Funk | trägerfrequenz f | radio carrier frequency
~ überlastung f | radio congestion
~ übertragung f | radio transmission
~ umfeld n | radio environment
~ verbindung f | radio link
~ verkehr m | radio traffic
~ verkehrsbereich m, Versorgungsbereich m, Dienstbereich m, Netzbereich m | service area

~ verkehrsbereich m, Bereich m einer Funkfeststation f, Basisstationsbereich m | base station area

~ vermittlungseinrichtung f, | mobile services switching center,
~ vermittlungsstelle f, | MSC, mobile switching center,
Mobilvermittlungsstelle f, | mobile exchange
Überleiteinrichtung f

besuchte ~ vermittlungsstelle f | visited mobile services switching center, visited MSC, visited exchange

~ vermittlungsstellenbereich m, | mobile services switching center
~ vermittlungsbereich m, | area, MSC area
Vermittlungsbereich m

~ versorgung f, ~ bedeckung f | radio coverage
~ versorgungsgebiet n, | radio coverage area
~ versorgungsbereich m

~ verwaltungskonferenz f, | World Administrative Radio Conference, WARC
Welt ~ verwaltungskonferenz f

~ weg m | radio path
~ wellen fpl | radio waves
~ zelle f | radio cell, radio zone, zone, cell
~ zone f | radio cell, radio zone
   benachbarte ~ zone f | adjacent radio cell, neighbouring cell
   überlagerte ~ zone f | overlaid cell
   unterlagerte ~ zone f | underlaid cell
   andere in Frage kommenden ~ zonen fpl | candidate cells

~ zonenabstand m   cell spacing
~ zonengrenze f   cell boundary
~ zonengruppe f   cluster
~ zonenkennung f   cell identity
~ zonenkonfiguration f   cell configuration
~ zonenradius m   cell radius (Plural: radii)
~ zonenspaltung f   cell splitting
~ zonenüberlagerung f   cell overlay, cell underlay
~ zonenunterteilung f   cell subdivision
~ zonenversorgungsbereich m   cell coverage area
~ zonenwechsel m   cell change
funkzonenweise   cell-by-cell
Funkzonenzuordnung f   cell placement
Fuzzy-Logik f, ,,unscharfe'' Logik f   fuzzy logic

G

Gabel f (Tel.)   cradle
~ schaltung f   hybrid, hybrid circuit
Ganz | glasfaser f (Lichtwellenleiter m)   all-glass fiber
~ wellendipol m   full-wave dipole
Gateway n (Verbindung f von ungleichen Netzen npl)   gateway
Gebiete npl   areas
    abgelegene ~   outlying areas
    bebaute ~   built-up areas
    erschlossene ~   developed areas
    ländliche ~   rural areas
    städtische ~   urban areas
Gebietsüberdeckung f   area coverage

Gebühr f	charge, call charge, rate, fee
einmalige ~	one-time charge, non-recurring charge
feste monatliche ~	fixed monthly charge
Gebühren | anzeige f	advice of charge, AOC, charge display
~ anzeiger m	charge indicator, charge meter
~ bemessung f (nach Dauer f)	charging by time
~ einheit f	traffic unit
~ erfassung f	call metering, charge metering, charge registration
gebührenfrei	free, non-chargeable, toll-free
~ e Nummer f	freephone service
~ er Anruf m	no-charge call
gebührengünstige Zeit f	low-charge period
Gebührenminuten fpl	chargeable minutes
gebührenpflichtig	chargeable, toll (call)
Gebühren | struktur f	charge structure
~ übernahme f	reversed charging
~ übernahme (durch gerufenen Teilnehmer m)	freephone service
~ verrechnung f	billing
~ zähler m	charge indicator, charge meter
~ zählung f	charge registration
~ zone f	charging area
~ zuschreiben n	notification of chargeable time
Gegen | amt n	distant operator, destination office
~ funkstelle f	called station, answering station
~ sprechanlage f	two-way intercom system
~ sprechen n, Duplex n	duplex
gehende Belegung f	outgoing seizure
Gelände n	terrain, area
nicht quasiebenes ~	irregular terrain
offenes ~	open areas
quasieebenes ~	quasi-smooth terrain
Gelände | daten f	topographical data
~ formation f	terrain type
~ merkmale npl	terrain features
gemeinsame Luftschnittstelle f	common air interface

Gemeinschaftsleitung f	party line, shared service line
Gentex-Dienst m (USA)	gentex (general telegraph exchange)
geostationärer Satellit m	geostationary satellite
Geradeaustest m	quick test, straight-forward test
Geräte | datei f	equipment identity register (EIR)
~ kennung f	device code
Geräuschabstand m	signal-to-noise ratio
Gesamtsystemstatus m	overall system status
geschlossene Benutzergruppe f	closed user group
Gespräch n	call
bestehendes ~, laufendes ~	call in progress
~ in Wartestellung f	camped-on call
Gesprächs | abwicklung f	call handling
~ anmeldung f	call booking
~ begrenzung f	call restriction
~ entgelt n	call fee
~ güte f	transmission performance
~ qualität f	speech quality, call quality
~ umschaltung f	handoff
~ verhalten n	calling pattern
~ weiterleitung f (bei Funk- zonenwechsel m)	automatic handoff
~ weiterverbindung f	call transfer
~ zähler m	call meter
~ zeit f	call duration, airtime
Gestört | zustand m	out-of-order condition
~ zeichen n	out-of-order tone
Gewinn m (Antenne f)	gain
gewünschtes Signal n	wanted signal
Glas | faser f (Lichtwellenleiter m)	optical fiber, glass fiber
~ faserkabel n	fiber optic cable
~ fasernetz n	optical fiber network
gleichberechtigt	with equality of access
Gleichkanal m	co-channel, common channel
Gleichkanal | abstand m, Gleich- kanal/-Wiederholabstand m	co-channel reuse distance

~-Basisstation f, ~ funkfeststation f	co-channel base station
~ betrieb m	co-channel operation
~ funkzone f	co-channel cell
~ schutzabstand m	co-channel protection ratio
~ störung f	co-channel interference
Gleich | laufsteuerung f	synchronization control
~ laufverfahren n	synchronization procedure
gleichstromfrei umcodieren	to convert (signals) with no dc component
Gleich | takt m	common mode
~ taktunterdrückung f	common-mode rejection
Gliederung f, funktionelle ~	functional organization
GMSK-Modulationsverfahren n	Gaussian minimum shift keying
GPIB (general purpose interface bus)	IEC-Bus (nach IEEE-Standard für Schnittstellenbusse)
Gradienten | profilfaser f	gradient index fiber
~ wellenleiter m	graded-index optical waveguide
Grobtakt m	coarse-time clock pulse
Groß/flächen-Funkstation f	umbrella site
~ leistungs-Basisstation f	high-power base station
~ rechner m	mainframe
~ zone f, ~ zelle f	large cell
Grund | dienste mpl	basic services, standard services
~ gebühr f	fixed charge, subscriber's rental
~ stellung f	home position
~ takt m	basic clock rate, basic pulse rate
~ übertragungsdämpfung f	basic transmission loss, basic propagation loss
~ welle f	ground wave
Gruppen | auswahl f	group selection
~ brechzahl f (Lichtwellenleiter m)	group index
~ koppler m	group switch
~ laufzeit f	group delay time
~ laufzeitverzerrung f	group delay distortion
~ ruf m	group paging, multi-party call
~ signalrahmen m	alarm signalling frame, group alarm frame

~ wähler m — group selector
~ wahl f — controlled hunting, group selection
Gruppierung f — trunking arrangement
GSM (Group Spéciale Mobile) — GSM (CEPT-Unterausschuß m für europäische digitale Mobilfunkdienste mpl)
GSM-Konformität f — GSM conformity
Gütezähler m — quality-of-service meter

halb | amtsberechtigte Nebenstelle f — limited-access extension
~ automatische Vermittlung f — semi-automatic switching
Halbduplex — half duplex
Halten einer Verbindung f — call hold
Hamming-Abstand m — Hamming distance
Hand | apparat m — handset
~ -Mobilstation f — handheld mobile station, handheld portable mobile station, hand-portable unit, hand-held portable radiotelephone
~ sprechfunkgerät n — hand-carried transceiver
~ telefon n, ~ held-Gerät n — handheld phone, handportable, handy
handvermitteltes Gespräch n — operator-assisted call, operator-initiated call
Haupt | anschluß m für Direktruf m, HfD — main station for fixed connection, leased data circuit terminal
~ sendezeit f — peak air time
~ takt m — master clock
~ verkehrsstunde f — busy hour, peak hour

angebotene Belegungen fpl in der ~ verkehrsstunde f
~ vermittlungsstelle f

Hauspost f, elektronische ~
HDLC (codeunabhängiges Steuerungsverfahren n)
Heimat | bereich m

~ datei f
~ -Funkvermittlung f,
~ -Funkvermittlungsstelle f
~ netz n
herabsetzen, mindern (z.B. Sprachqualität f)
herstellen (Verbindung f)
Heterodyn-Empfang m
HF-Störabstand m
Hilfs | kanal m
~ trägermodulation f
Hinter | grundnetz n
~ grundtest m
Hin- und Rückwegverzögerung f
Hinweis/-Ansagegerät n
~ gabe f (ankommende Sperre f mit Zuschreiben eines Textes m)
~ ton m
Hochfrequenzkanal m, HF-Kanal m
hochladen
Hoch | paß m
~ seekabel n
Höhenstruktur f
höheres Protokoll n

busy hour call attempts, BHCA

main exchange, primary exchange, regional switch

electronic in-house mail
HDLC (high level data link control)

home mobile services switching center area, home MSC area, home region
home location register, HLR
home mobile services switching center, home MSC, home exchange
home public land mobile network
to degrade (speech quality)

to establish, to set up (a call)
heterodyne reception
RF signal-to-interference ratio
backward channel
subcarrier modulation
backbone network
background test
roundtrip delay
short-text announcer
customer-recorded information, notification for receiver
alerting tone
RF channel, radio frequency channel
to upload
high-pass filter
deepsea cable
topographical structure
higher-level protocol

51

Hörer m	receiver, handset
~ abgenommen	off hook
~ aufgelegt	on hook
Wahl f bei aufliegendem ~	on-hook dialling
Hör | kapsel f	receiver inset, earphone
~ ton m	call-progress tone, CPT
~ tonzeitlage f	tone time slot
Hohlleiter m	waveguide
Homing-Verfahren f	homing method
Hornparabolantenne f	horn-reflector antenna
Hot | -line-Service m	hot-line service
~ -standby-Verfahren n	hot-standby method

I

IBFN (integriertes breitbandiges Fernmeldenetz n)	integrated broadband telecommunications network
Identifizierung f bösartiger Anrufe mpl	malicious call identification, MCI
~ der gerufenen Leitung f	called line identification
~ der rufenden Leitung f	calling line identification
IDN (integriertes Text- und Datennetz n)	integrated digital network
IEC (internationale Normungsorganisation f auf dem Gebiet n der Elektrotechnik f)	IEC (International Electrotechnical Commission)
IEEE (Verband m der Elektroingenieure mpl und Elektrotechniker mpl, USA)	IEEE (Institute of Electrical and Electronics Engineers)
Imband-Signalisierung f	in-band signalling

Impuls m	pulse
Kosinusquadrat-~	raised-cosine pulse
Impuls | gabe f	pulsing
~ wahl f	pulse signalling
Individualkommunikation f	individual communication
individuelle Kurzwahl f	personalized speed calling
Indiz n	error symptom
Informations | anbieter m (Btx)	information provider
~ dienst m	information service
~ rahmen m	information frame
~ umkehr f	signal wraparound
~ vergleicher m	information comparator
Infrastruktur f	infrastructure
Inlands | -Fernvermittlungsstelle f	national trunk exchange
~ verkehr m	national traffic, domestic traffic
innere Blockierung f	internal blocking
Institut n für Europäische Telekommunikationsstandards mpl	European Telecommunications Standards Institute, ETSI
Integration f,	
betriebs- und sicherungstechnische ~	administration, maintenance and dependability integration
vermittlungstechnische ~	call-processing integration
integriertes Text- und Datennetz n, IDN	integrated text and data network
INTELSAT (internationaler Fernmeldesatellit m)	INTELSAT (International Telecommunication Satellite)
Interferenz f,	
elektromagnetische ~	electromagnetic interference, EMI
interkontinentaler Fernsprechverkehr m	intercontinental telephone traffic
Inter | modulation f	intermodulation
~ modulationsstörung f	intermodulation interference
Internationaler beratender Ausschuß f für den Funkdienst m	International Radio Consultative Committee (CCIR)
internationale Durchgangsvermittlungsstelle f	international transit exchange
~ Gerätekennung f	international mobile station equipment identity, IMEI

53

~ Kopfamt n   international gateway exchange, international gateway center

~ Teilnehmerkennung f   international mobile subscriber identity, IMSI

~ Zugangskennzahl f   international prefix

Intern | umschaltung f   intracell handoff, intracell handover, intrahandoff, intra-zone channel reassignment

~ verbindung f   intra-exchange call

Interzonen-Weiterreichen n   inter-cell handover

Intrazonen-Weiterreichen n   intra-cell handover

ISDN (diensteintegrierendes digitales Netz)   integrated services digital network

~ -Nebenstellenanlage f   ISDN PABX

~ -Teilnehmeranschluß m   ISDN user basic access

ISO (internationales Normungsgremium n)   ISO (International Organization for Standardization)

ISO/OSI-Referenzmodell n (OSI-Schichtenmodell n) (OSI = Kommunikation f offener Systeme npl)   ISO/OSI reference model, layer model OSI (Open Systems Interconnection)

isotrope Antenne f   isotropic antenna

J

Jedermann-Funk m   citizens' band radio, CB radio

Jitterreduzierer m   jitter reducer

K

Kanal m	channel
benachbarter ~	adjacent channel
festgeschalteter ~	dedicated channel
zentraler ~	common channel
~ mit halber Bitrate f	half-rate channel
Kanal | abgleichung f	channel alignment
~ abstand m, Nachbar ~ abstand	channel spacing
~ anreiz m	channel event
~ ausstattung f, ~ einteilung f	channelization
~ bündel n	channel group, channel set
~ bündelung f	trunking
~ durchschaltung f	channel switching
kanalindividuelle Zeichengabe f	channel-associated signalling
Kanal | kapazität f	channel capacity
~ nebensprechen n	interchannel crosstalk
~ sprung m	transfer in channel
~ teilung f	multiple use of channels
~ zustandsbit n	channel status bit
~ zuteilung f	channel assignment
bedarfsweise ~ zuteilung f	demand assignment
feste ~ zuteilung f	fixed channel assignment
flexible ~ zuteilung f	flexible channel assignment
Kantenbeugung f	knife-edge diffraction
Karenzzeit f	non-chargeable interval
Kartentelefon n	card telephone, chip-card telephone
Katastrophenberechtigung f	catastrophe privilege, catastrophe class of service

Kennung f | identification, identity
~ der Basisstation f | base station code, base station identity code, BSIC

Kennungs | austausch m, Kennungstausch m | exchange of identifications, exchange of identification codes, answerback exchange
~ prüfung f | answerback verification

Kenn | wort n | password, keyword, code
~ ziffer f | code digit, prefix

Kerndurchmesser m (Lichtwellenleiter m) | core diameter

Kettung f von Leistungsmerkmalen npl | chaining of features

Klassenkennzeichnung f | class-of-service code

Kleinleistungs-Basisstation f | low-power base station

Kleinstzone f, Mikrozelle f | microcell

Kleinzelle f | small cell

Klirren n | harmonic distortion

Klirrfaktor m | harmonic distortion factor

Knacken n | click

Knack | rate f | click rate
~ störung f | click noise

Knoten | rechner m | node, node computer
~ vermittlungsstelle f | main switch

Koaxialkabel n, Koax-Kabel | coaxial cable, coax cable

Kohärenzbandbreite f | coherence bandwidth

Kollision f, Konflikt m | collision

Kollisionserkennung f, | collision detection
  Mehrfachzugriff m mit ~ | carrier sense multiple access with collision detection, CSMA/CD

Komfort | betriebsterminal n | enhanced-feature service terminal
~ telefon n | added-feature telephone

Kommunikation f offener Systeme npl | open system interconnection, OSI
  diensteüberschreitende ~ | interservice communication
  netzüberschreitende ~ | internetwork communication
  nichtsprachliche ~ | non-voice communication

Kommunikationsprotokoll n	communication protocol
Kompakttelefon n	compact telephone
Kompander m	compander
Kompatibilität f	compatibility
komprimieren	to compress
Konferenz │ gespräch n, Telefon-Konferenz f	conference calling
~schaltung f	conference circuit, conference service
~verbindung f	conference call, conference connection
~verstärker m	conference repeater
Konfigurationsänderung f	reconfiguration
Konflikt m	contention
~auflösung f	contention control
Konformitätsbescheinigung f	certificate of conformity
Konkurrenzbetrieb	contention mode
kontinuierliche Phasen-Frequenz-Umtastung f	continuous phase frequency shift keying, CPFSK
Konvertierungsdienste mpl	conversion services
Konvolutionscodierung f	convolutional coding
Konzentrator m	concentrator
Kopf │ amt n	gateway exchange
~stelle f	head end
Koppel │ feld n, Koppelnetz n	switching network
blockierungsfreies ~	non-blocking switching network
~matrix f, ~vielfach n	switching matrix
Koppler-Mobilvermittlungsstelle f	gateway mobile switching center
Korrekturfaktor m	correction factor
Korrelations │ bandbreite f	correlation bandwidth
~eigengeräusch n	correlation self-noise
~empfang m	correlation detection
~faktor m, ~koeffizient m	correlation coefficient
Kosinusquadrat-Impuls m	raised-cosine pulse
Kreditkartengespräch n	credit-card call
Kreuz │ korrelationskoeffizient m	cross correlation coefficient
~modulation f	cross modulation

künstliche Störungen fpl   man-made noise

kumulative Verteilung f   cumulative distribution

Kurz | belegung f   short occupation
~ mitteilungsdienst m   short message service
~ nachricht f, ~ telegramm n   short message
~ rufnummer f   speed dialling code
~ speicher m   short-time storage
~ streckenmittelwert m   local mean
~ wahl f   speed dialling, short dialling, abbreviated dialling
   individuelle ~ wahl f   personalized speed dialling
~ wahlzeichen n   abbreviated dial code, abbreviated directory number
~ wellenfunk m   short-range radio
~ zeitarchivierung f   short-term filing
~ zeitmedianwert m   short-term median

L

LAN [lokales Netz(werk n)]   LAN (Local Area Network)
   geschlossenes ~   closed LAN
   offenes ~   open LAN

Landesfernwahlnetz n   national long-distance dialling network, national DDD network

Land | funk m   land radio
   beweglicher ~ funk m   land mobile radio
   beweglicher ~ funkdienst m   land mobile radio service
   bewegliche ~ funkstelle f   land mobile station
   öffentlicher beweglicher ~ funkdienst m   public land mobile service, PLMS
   öffentliches mobiles ~ funknetz n   public land mobile network, PLMN
~ zentrale f   rural exchange

Lang | rufnummer f	unabbreviated call number
~ streckenmedianwert m	large area median, large area median value
~ zeitmedianwert m	long-term median
Last | ausgleich m	load balancing
~ teilung f	load sharing
~ teilverfahren n	call load sharing mode
~ verteilung f	call load sharing
Laut | hören n	open listening, loud hearing operation
~ sprecherdurchsage f	loudspeaker announcement
Leistungs | dichtespektrum n	spectral power density
~ fähigkeit f	traffic handling capacity, call handling capacity
~ gewinn m (Antenne f)	gain
~ merkmale mpl (Dienste mpl)	features
erweiterte ~ merkmale mpl	enhanced features
~ pegel m	power level
~ regelung f	power control
Leit | befehl m	routing command
~ funkstelle f	radio control station
~ informationen fpl	switching information, routing information
~ steuerung f	primary control
Leitung f	circuit, link, line
festgeschaltete ~	dedicated circuit
~ in Multiplexschaltung f	multiplexed line
verlustlose ~	zero-loss circuit
Leitungs | abfrage f	line scan(ning)
~ art f	trunk type
~ ausnutzungsgrad m	line utilization degree
~ belegung f	line seizure
~ bündel n	trunk group, line group
gemeinsames ~ bündel n	common trunk group
Leitungscode m	line code
AMI-Code m	alternate mark inversion code
HDBn-Code m	high density bipolar code
NRZ-Code m	non-return-to-zero code
RZ-Code m	return-to-zero code

Leitungs | freigabe f — line enable
~ konzentrator m — line concentrator
~ notiz f — line scratchpad entry
  wechselseitiger ~ satz m — trunk circuit bothways
~ schicht f — data link layer
~ schnittstelle f — line interface
~ -Server m — line server
~ suchverfahren n — line hunting method
leitungsvermittelt — circuit-switched
~ e Dienste mpl — switched services
~ e Verbindung f — switched connection
~ es Netz n — switched network
~ es öffentliches Datennetz n — circuit-switched public data network, CSPDN

Leitungs | vermittlung f — circuit switching, CS
~ zugangsverfahren n — line-access procedure
~ zustandsmeldung f — line status signal

Leit | weg m — route
~ weglenkung f — routing, traffic routing
~ wegsteuerung f — routing control

Letztweg m — final route, last-choice route

Licht | leitstrecke f — optical link
~ leittechnik f — fiber optics
~ wellenleiter m — optical waveguide, optical fiber
~ wellenleiterkabel n — fiber optic cable, optical fiber cable, optical waveguide cable
~ wellenleitertechnik f — fiber optics, optical waveguide technology

Löschen n von Nachrichten fpl — erase message, message cancellation

Löschungs | anforderung f — cancellation request
~ vollzug m — cancellation completed

Lokalbetrieb m, ungestörter ~ — undisturbed local operation

lokales Breitbandnetz n — local area wideband network, wideband LAN

lokales Netzwerk n — local area network, LAN

Lokalisierung f, automatische ~ — automatic tracking

Luftschnittstelle f — radio interface, air interface
  gemeinsame ~ — common air interface

M

Mäanderfolge f	timing pulse train
Magnetfeldkoppler m	magnetic-field switching matrix
Mailbox f	mailbox
Makeln n	broker's call
~ bei der Abfragestelle f	two-way splitting
~ zwischen Abfrageorganen npl	alternating between call keys
Makrosprache f, vermittlungstechnische ~	switching-oriented macro language
markieren	to mark
Massenkommunikation f	mass communication
Maximumintegration f (ISDN)	maximum integration
Mehr | bereichsantenne f	multiband antenna
~ dienstebetrieb m	multiservice operation
~ dienste-Endgerät n	multiservice terminal
mehrfach ausnutzen	to multiplex
~ genutztes Netz n	multiservice network
Mehrfach | abtastung f	multiple scanning
~ anreiz m	multiple event
~ anschlußprozedur f	multi-link procedure
~ empfang m, Diversity-Empfang m	diversity reception
~ -Frequenzumtastung f	multiple frequency shift keying, MFSK
~ zugriff m mit Kollisionserkennung f	carrier sense multiple access with collision detection, CSMA/CD
Mehr | frequenzcode m	multi-frequency code
~ frequenzsignalisierung f	multi-frequency signalling
~ frequenzwahlverfahren n	dual tone multi-frequency signalling
~ funktionsmodem n	multi-function modem

~ kanaldurchschaltung f — multichannel switching
~ kanal-Modem n — multichannel modem
~ modenfaser f — multi-mode fiber
~ punktnetz n — multipoint network
~ punktverbindung f — multipoint connection
~ punktzugriff m — multipoint access

mehrstufiges Netz n — multistage network

Mehr | wegeausbreitung f — multipath propagation
~ wegeführung f — redundant routing
~ wegekanal m — multipath channel
~ wegemodell n — multipath model
~ wegeschwund m — multipath fading
~ wegesignal n — multipath signal
~ wertdienste mpl — value-added services, enhanced services
~ zweckschnittstelle f — general interface

Melde | aufruf m — location registration request
~ impuls m — answer pulse

Melden n — answering

Melde | signal n — answer signal
~ verzug m — answering delay
~ wartezeit f — ringing length

Meldung f — status signal, status message
  vermittlungstechnische ~ — call-processing message

Meldungs | lenkung f — message routing
~ verteilung f — message discrimination

Merkmal n (Dienste mpl, Leistungen fpl) — feature

Meßstation f, mobile ~ — mobile measurement unit

Messung f von Belegungszahlen fpl — peg count

Meßwert-Fernübertragung f — telemetering, telemetry

Miet | gebühr f — rental
~ leitung f — leased line, leased circuit
  internationale ~ leitung f — international leased circuit

Mikrofonlautsprecher m — talk-back loudspeaker

Mikro | wellenteilstrecke f	microwave radio hop
~ wellenverbindung f	microwave link
~ zelle f, Kleinstzone f	microcell
~ zellentechnik f	microcell technology
mindern, herabsetzen (z.B. Sprachqualität f)	to degrade (speech quality)
Mindest | feldstärke f	minimum usable field strength
~ versorgungsgrad m	minimum coverage rate
Misch | code m	mixed code
~ kommunikation f	mixed communications, mixed-mode communications
mitbenutzen	to share
mithören	to listen in, to monitor
Mittelwert m, örtlicher ~	local mean
Mittenfrequenz f	mid-frequency
mittlerer Ausfallabstand m	mean time between failures, MTBF
mobiles Funktelefon n	mobile radio telephone
~ r Teilnehmer m	mobile subscriber, mobile user
Mobil | funk m	mobile radio
~ funkbenutzerteil n	mobile user part
~ funkdienst m	mobile radio service, mobile phone service, radio-based mobile phone service, mobile radio telephone service
~ funkgeräte npl	mobile radio equipment, mobile equipment
~ funkkanal m	mobile radio channel
öffentliches ~ funknetz n	public land mobile network, PLMN
~ funkteilnehmer	mobile subscriber, mobile radio user
~ funkteilnehmernummer f, Funktelefonnummer f	mobile subsriber number
~ kommunikationssystem n	mobile communication system
~ station f	mobile station, mobile services station, MS
bewegliche ~ station f	transportable mobile station
fahrzeuggebundene ~ station	vehicular mobile station
tragbare ~ station	portable mobile station
~ stationsleistungsmerkmal n	mobile station feature

~ station-Basisstation-Schnittstelle f | mobile-station-to-base-station interface
~ telefon n | mobile radio telephone, mobile telephone
~ vermittlungsstelle f, Überleiteinrichtung f, Funkvermittlungsstelle f | mobile services switching center, mobile switching center, MSC
Modem m | modem (modulator/demodulator)
~ strecke f | modem link
Modul m (Baugruppe f) | module
modulare Netzstruktur f | modular network structure
Modulbetriebstechnik f | module administration and maintenance
Modulationsverfahren n | modulation method
modulieren, auf eine Trägerfrequenz ~ | to modulate to a carrier frequency
Modulsicherheitstechnik f | module dependability system
Modus m, Moden pl (Lichtwellenleiter m) | mode, modes
Momentanfeldstärke f | instantaneous field strength
Monomodefaser f, Einmodenfaser | single-mode fiber, monomode fiber
Münzer m, Münzfernsprecher m | paystation, coinbox telephone, payphone
Münzerkennung f | coin validation
Multi | blockverfahren n | multi-frame mode
~ funktionsterminal n | multifunction terminal
~ modenfaser | multimode fiber
Multiplex n auflösen | to demultiplex
Multiplexer m, Mux | multiplexer
Multiplex-Schnittstelle f, Mux-Schnittstelle f | multiplex interface
Multiprozessorbetrieb m | multiprocessor mode
Musikeinspielung f im Haltezustand m, Beruhigungston m | music on hold
Mutteramt n | parent exchange

N

Nachbar | amt n — adjacent exchange
~ bereich m — adjacent area
~ funkzone f — adjacent cell
~ funkfeststation f, benachbarte Basisstation f — adjacent base station
~ kanal m — adjacent channel
   Störung f durch den ~ kanal — adjacent-channel interference
~ kanalabstand m, Kanalabstand m — channel spacing
~ kanaldämpfung f — adjacent-channel attenuation
~ kanalselektivität f — adjacent-channel selectivity
~ kanalstörung f — adjacent-channel interference
~ zeichenstörung f — intersymbol interference, ISI
~ zelle f — adjacent cell, neighbouring cell

Nachrichten | behandlung — message handling
~ block m — message block
~ fernschaltgerät n — network termination unit
~ inhalt m — message content, information content
~ kanal m — traffic channel, TCH
~ satellit m (z.B. INTELSAT) — communications satellite
~ -Speichervermittlungsstelle f — message switching center, store-and-forward switching center
~ technik f — (tele)communications technology
~ übermittlung f (= Nachrichtenübertragung f + Nachrichtenvermittlung f) — transmission and switching of information

~ verkehr m — message traffic
~ verkettung f — message chaining

Nachrufen n — re-ringing, ring-back

Nachrufzeichen n — re-ringing signal, ring-back signal

Nachtkonzentration f	restricted night service
Nachwahl f	suffix dialling
Nah | bereichszone f	local fee zone
~ nebensprechdämpfung f	near-end crosstalk attenuation
~ tarif m	local tariff
~ verkehr m	short-distance traffic, short-haul traffic
Namenstaste f für Kurzwahl f	name key for speed dialling
nationales Roaming	national roaming
nationale Rufnummer f	national terminal number
naturgegebene Funkstörung f	natural noise
Neben | anschluß m	extension line
~ aussendungen fpl	spurious emissions
~ sprechdämpfung f	crosstalk attenuation
~ sprechen, Übersprechen n	crosstalk
~ stelle f	extension
halbamtsberechtigte ~ stelle	indirect-access extension, limited-access extension, partially restricted extension
nicht amtsberechtigte ~ stelle f	no-access extension, completely restricted extension
voll amtsberechtigte ~ stelle f	unrestricted extension
private automatische ~ stellenanlage f	private automatic branch exchange, PABX
private ~ stellenanlage	private branch exchange, PBX
private digitale ~ stellenanlage	private digital exchange, PDX
~ stellenapparat m	extension set
~ ton m	sidetone
Netz n	network
dienstspezifisches ~	service-specific network
eigenständiges ~	dedicated network
flächendeckendes ~	full-coverage network
gemischt strukturiertes ~	mixed structure network
homogenes ~	homogeneous network
integriertes digitales ~	integrated digital network, IDN
leitungsvermitteltes ~	circuit-switched network
paketvermitteltes ~	packet-switched network
~ mit erweiterten Übertragungsmöglichkeiten fpl	value-added network

| ~ mit Mehrfachnutzung f, mehrfach genutztes ~ | multi-service network |

netzabhängig network-dependent

Netz | abschluß m	network termination
~ abschlußgerät n	network termination unit
~ anpassungseinrichtung f	interworking equipment, interworking unit
~ anschlußtechnik f	network interfacing, network interface technology
~ architektur f	network architecture
~ aufbau m	network construction, network establishment
~ ausbau m	network expansion
~ ausfallüberwachung f	power control
~ ausfallüberwachungsmeldung f	power control message
~ bereich m, Dienstbereich m	service area
~ betreiber m	network operator
~ betrieb m	network operation
~ diagnose f	network diagnosis
~ dienst m	network service
~ dienstleistungen fpl für Mehrwertdienste mpl	value-added networks services, VANS
~ ebene f	network level
~ entwurf m	network design
~ erweiterung f	network extension
~ fehlermeldung f	network failure report
~ führung f	network management
~ knoten m	network node
~ konfiguration f	network configuration
~ koppler m	gateway
~ leistungsmerkmal n	network feature
~ meldung f	network message
~ -Netz-Schnittstelle f	internetwork interface
~ software f	network software
~ störung f	network failure
zellulare ~ struktur f	cellular network structure
~ takt m	network clock pulse, network timing pulse

~ topologie f, ~ struktur f | network topology
~ übergang m | network interworking
~ übergänge mpl | network interconnections
~ überlastung f | network congestion
netzüberschreitende Kommunikation f | internetwork communication

Netz | verkehrssteuerung f | network traffic control
~ verwaltung f | network management, network administration
~ verwaltungssteuerung f | network management control system
~ verwaltungszentrale f | network management center, NMC
~ (werk)protokoll n | network protocol
~ werkprozessor m | network processor
~ werkschicht f | network layer
~ zugang m | network access
~ zusammenbruch m | system collapse, black-out

Neuversuch m (bei Besetztzustand m) | reattempt (on busy)

NF-Schutzabstand m | AF protection ratio
~ -Störabstand m | AF signal-to-interference ratio

Nicht-Fernsprechdienst m | non-voice service

Nichtsprachdienst m | non-voice service

nichtsprachliche Kommunikation f | non-voice communication

nicht verfügbare Zeit f | unavailable time

~ zustellbare Nachricht f | non-deliverable message

Notruf | dienst m | emergency call service
~ stelle f | emergency call station
~ telefon n | emergency telephone
~ träger m | emergency organization

NTG (Nachrichtentechnische Gesellschaft im Verband Deutscher Elektrotechniker VDE e.V.)

Nullstellung f, Suchverfahren n mit ~ | search with homing

Nummern | schalterimpuls m | dial pulse
~ schalterwahl f | number plate dialling

Teilnehmer m mit ~ schalterwahl f	dialplate subscriber
~ scheibe f	dialplate, number plate
~ scheibenimpuls m	dial pulse
NU-Ton m (NU = Nummer f unbeschaltet)	number-unobtainable tone, NU tone
Nur-Ton-Funkrufdienst m	tone-only paging
Nutz | feldstärke f	signal strength, usable field strength
~ kanal m	user signal channel, speech/data channel, desired channel
~ signal n	desired signal, useful signal

Ober | band n	upper half band
~ flächenwellenfilter n	surface wave filter
öffentliches analoges Fernsprechwählnetz n	automatic analog public telephone network
~ er beweglicher Landfunkdienst m	public mobile telephone service
~ es bewegliches Landfunknetz n	public mobile radio network
~ es Datennetz n	public data network
~ er Datenübermittlungsdienst m	public data transmission service
~ es Direktrufnetz n	public leased-circuit data network
~ es Fernsprechnetz n	public telephone network
~ es Fernsprechwählnetz n	general switched telephone network
~ es Selbstwählferndienstnetz n	public switched telephone network, PSTN
~ es Vermittlungsnetz n	public switched network
~ es Wählnetz n	public switched network
offene Kommunikation f	open systems communications

optisches Anklopfen n	optical call-waiting indication, visual camp-on
optische Fernmeldetechnik f	optical telecommunications
~ Nachrichtentechnik f	optical communications technology
~ Signalisierung f	visual signalling
örtlicher Ablauffehler m	local procedure error
~ Mittelwert m	local mean
Organisation f, betriebstechnische ~	administration and maintenance organization
Orts | amt n	local exchange, local switching center
~ bereich m	local area, local service area
ortsbeweglich, ortsveränderbar	
(fahrbar)	mobile
(tragbar)	portable
(transportierbar)	transportable
Ortsdurchgangsvermittlung f	local tandem exchange
ortsfest	fixed, landline, stationary
~e Funkstelle f	land station
~ Landfunkstelle f, Funkfeststation f, Basisstation	base station, BS, fixed station
Orts | gebühr f	local rate, local call fee
~ gespräch n	local call
~ knoten m	local node
~ netz n	local network
~ netzkennzahl f	area code
~ (netz)teilnehmer m	local subscriber
~ registrierung f, Standortregistrierung f	location registration
~ verbindung f	local call
~ verbindungsnetz n	local communication network
~ verkehr m	local traffic
~ vermittlungsstelle f	local switch, local exchange, local switching center, local office
Ortungsdienst m für gestohlene Fahrzeuge npl	stolen vehicle locator service
Orts | zeituhr f	local time clock
~ zone f	local zone

OSI (Kommunikation f offener Systeme npl) — OSI (Open Systems Interconnection)
~-Referenzmodell n — OSI reference model, layer model
Ozeankabel n — submarine cable

P

Paket n — packet
~betrieb m, ~modus m — packet mode
~fehlerwahrscheinlichkeit f — packet error probability
~format n — packet format
Paketierer-/Depaketierer-Einrichtung f, PAD — packet assembly | disassembly facility
Paketierung f — packet assembly
Paketnetz n — packet network
paketorientierte Zugangsprozedur f — packet-oriented access procedure
Paketteilnehmer m — packet-terminal subscriber
paketvermitteltes Netz — packet-switched network
Paket | vermittlung f — packet switching
~vermittlungsamt n — packet-switching exchange
~vermittlungsnetz n — packet-switching network
~vermittlungsprozedur f — packet-switching procedure
paketweise Nachrichtenübermittlung f — packet-oriented transmission of messages
Paketwiederholung f — packet retransmission
papierloses Büro n — paperless office, paper-free office
Parabolantenne f — parabolic antenna, dish antenna
Parallelruf m — parallel ringing
parasitäre Aussendungen fpl — parasitic emissions

Parken n (einer Verbindung f)	call parking
Parkschaltung f	call park
Partnerleitung f	serving line, serving port
Pauschaltarif m	flat rate
Pausen | zeichensteuerung f	pause signal control
~ zeit f	interval, pause
PCM-30-Zeitmultiplexsystem	PCM-30 time division multiplex system (PCM = pulse code modulation)
PCN (individuelles Kommunikationsnetz n)	PCN (personal communication network)
Pegel m	level
~ sprung m	level discontinuity
Peilanzeige f	bearing indication
Peilung f	direction finding
Peitschenantenne f	whip antenna
Pendlerverhalten n	commuting pattern
Peripherie f, vermittlungstechnische ~	call-processing periphery, switching-oriented periphery, peripheral switching equipment
persönliche Kennummer f	personal identification number, PIN
~ Rufnummer f	personal call number
personenbezogene Berechtigung f	personal authorization
~ e Daten f	personal data
personenorientierte Rufnummer f	personalized call number
Personen | ruf m	paging
~ rufanlage f, ~ suchanlage f	paging system
Pfadsteuerung f	path control
Phasen | differenzumtastung f	differential phase shift keying, DPSK
~ -Frequenz-Umtastung f, kontinuierliche ~ Frequenzumtastung f	continuous phase frequency shift keying, CPFSK
~ jitter n	phase jitter
~ mittlung f	phase averaging
~ modulation, PM	phase modulation

~ schwund m	phase fading
differentielle ~ sprung-modulation f	differential phase shift keying, DPSK
~ umtastung f	phase shift keying, PSK
Piepston m	beep
Pilot | empfänger m	pilot receiver
~ ton m	pilot tone
Platzbeteiligung f	operator assistance
platzvermittelte Verbindung f	operator-assisted call, operator-initiated call
Polarisations-Diversity	polarization diversity
Poolbelegung f	pool capacity utilized
Postfach n, elektronisches ~	electronic mailbox
Prinzip n ,,rufender Teilnehmer m zahlt"	"calling party pays" principle
Platzanforderung f	request for operator service
Prioritätenaustausch m	priority exchange
Priorität f für abgehende/ankommende Rufe mpl	outgoing/incoming priority
Prioritätsanzeige f	precedence indicator
privilegierter Betrieb m	privileged operation
Programmanforderung f	program request
Programmiersprache f, vermittlungstechnisch orientierte ~	switching-oriented programming language
Protokoll n	protocol
höheres ~	higher-level protocol
Protokoll | architektur f	protocol architecture
~ ebene f, ~ schicht f	protocol layer
~ norm f	protocol standard
~ wandler m	protocol converter
Prozedur f	procedure, protocol
aufgerufene ~	invoked procedure
aufrufende ~	invoking procedure
Prozedurschnittstelle f	procedure interface

Prozessor m für Signali-　　　　　data communication link
　sierungssteuerung f

Prüf | bündel n　　　　　　　　test line group, testing trunk group
~ muster n　　　　　　　　　　test pattern

Puls | amplitudenmodulation f　　pulse amplitude modulation, PAM
~ codemodulation f　　　　　　pulse code modulation, PCM
~ frequenzmodulation f　　　　　pulse frequency modulation, PFM
~ phasenmodulation f　　　　　pulse phase modulation, PPM
~ zeitmodulation f　　　　　　　pulse time modulation

Punktverbindung f　　　　　　point-to-point connection

Punkt-zu-Mehrpunkt-ISDN-Ver-　point-to-multipoint ISDN connection
　bindung f

Q

Quantisierung f　　　　　　　　quantization, quantizing

Quantisierungs | geräusch n　　　quantization noise, quantization distortion

~ intervall n　　　　　　　　　　quantizing interval

Quarzglasfaser f (Licht-　　　　silica-glass fiber
　wellenleiter m)

Quer | strahler m　　　　　　　broadside array
~ verbindungsleitung f　　　　　tie line, tie trunk

quittieren　　　　　　　　　　　to acknowledge

Quittierung f, Quittung f　　　　acknowledgement
　negative ~　　　　　　　　　negative acknowledgement, NAK
　positive ~　　　　　　　　　positive acknowledgement, ACK
　Dialog mit ~　　　　　　　　acknowledged interaction

Quittierungsgabe f zum　　　　acknowledgement to originator
　Absender m

Quittungs | austausch m, Quittungsbetrieb m	acknowledgement, handshaking, handshake
~ freigabe f	acknowledgement enable signal
~ signal n	acknowledge signal
Quotieren n	quota-based allocation of traffic, quota-based distribution of traffic
Quotierungstabelle f	call quota allocation table

Radiostummschaltung f	automatic muting feature
Radom n (Antennenschutz m)	radome
Rahmen m	frame
~ dauer f	frame duration
~ länge f	frame length
~ synchronisierung f, adaptive ~	adaptive frame alignment
~ takt m	frame clock, frame pulsing
~ wiederherstellung f	reframing
Raster m	signalling pattern
~ verzerrung f	timing error
räumliches Verkehrsaufkommen n	spatial traffic demand
Raum | diversity	space diversity
~ multiplexverfahren n	space-division multiplex method
~ vielfachverbindung f	space-division multiplex connection
Rauschabstand m	signal-to-noise ratio, SNR
Rauschen n, Geräusch n	noise
Rausch | faktor m	noise factor
~ grenze f	noise threshold
~ unempflindlichkeit f	noise immunity

~verhalten n	noise performance
Rayleigh/-Kriterium n	Rayleigh criterion
~-Schwund m, Kurzzeitschwund m	Rayleigh fading, short-term fading
~-Verteilung f	Rayleigh distribution
rechnergesteuerte Vermittlungsstelle f	computer-controlled exchange
Redundanz f	redundancy
~prüfung f	redundancy check
Reflexion f, diffuse ~	diffuse reflection
Reflexions | faktor m	reflection coefficient
~winkel m (Lichtwellenleiter m)	angle of reflection
Regel | steilheit f	control slope
~verkehr m	regular routing
Reichweite f	radio coverage, service area, coverage, range
die ~ verlassen	to pass out of range
vermittlungstechnische ~	switching range
Rekonfiguration f	reconfiguration
Relais | koppelfeld n	relay switching matrix
~satellit m	repeater satellite
Reservebetrieb m	backup mode, standby mode
Resonanzreflektor m	resonating reflector
Restverkehr m	residual traffic, overflow traffic
R-Gespräch n	reverse charging, collect call
Richt | antenne f	directional antenna
~funk m	radio relay system
~funkstrecke f	radio link
~funkteilstrecke f	microwave radio hop
Richtungs | ausscheidungsziffer f	route discriminating digit
~wähler m	route selector
Ring | netz n	ring network
~struktur f	ring configuration
~topologie f	ring topology
Roamer-Verrechnungsstelle f	roamer clearing house
Roaming, Wandern n (freier	roaming

Rufbereichswechsel m)	
~-Nummer f	mobile station roaming number, MSRN
Rotations | parabolantenne f	parabolic-disk antenna
~ paraboloid n	paraboloid of revolution
Rück | frage f	consultation, hold for inquiry
~ frageeinrichtung f	refer-back facility
rückfragen	to call back
Rückfrage-Teilnehmerschaltung f	consultation line circuit
Rück | hördämpfung f	sidetone suppression
~ hörgeräusch n	sidetone
~ kanal m	backward channel
~ meldepriorität f	acknowledgement priority
~ meldung f	acknowledgement, acknowledge message, feedback
negative ~ meldung f	negative acknowledgement, NAK
positive ~ meldung f	positive acknowledgement, ACK
rückpolen	to restore polarity
Rück | ruf m	callback, ringback
~ ruf im Besetztfall m	callback on busy (completion of calls to busy subscribers)
~ rufauftrag m	callback request
~ rufverbindung f	callback connection, ringback connection
~ rufweg m	callback path
rücksetzen	to reset
Rücksetzzusammenstoß m	reset collision
Rückstrahldämpfung f	front-to-end ratio
Ruf m	call
abgehender ~	call request, outgoing call
ankommender ~	incoming call
nicht zur Verbindung führender ~	lost call
~ ohne Wahl f	non-dialled call
~ wiederholen	to re-ring
Ruf | abweisung f	call-not-accepted signal
~ abwicklung f	call handling

~ anforderung f — call request
~ annahme f — call-accepted signal
~ anzahlüberschreitung f — call rate overflow
~ aufbauprozedur f — call setup procedure
~ aufbauzeit f — call set-up time
~ bereich m — paging area
   Funk ~ bereich m — calling area
~ daten pl — call data
~ empfänger m — pager

rufen — to call, to ring, to page

Ruf | erkennung f — call detection, call identification
~ kanal m — calling channel, paging channel, PCH
~ leistung f — new-call rate
~ leitweglenkung f — call routing
~ nummer f — call number, subscriber's number, directory number
~ nummer f besetzt — number busy
   personenorientierte ~ nummer — personalized call number
~ nummernanzeige f — call number display
~ nummernspeicher m — call number memory
~ pause f — ring pause
~ signal n — ringing signal, paging signal
~ ton m (vorwärts) — ringing tone
   (rückwärts) — ringback tone
~ umleitung f — call diversion
~ warteschlange f — ringing queue
   automatische ~ wiederholung f — automatic retry
~ zeichen n — ringing signal
~ zusammenstoß m — call collision

Ruhe f vor dem Telefon n — do-not-disturb service feature

Rund | hohlleiter m — circular waveguide
~ schreibbetrieb m — multi-address operation
~ senden n — multi-address service
~ senden n und Verteilen n — multi-address call/distribution feature
~ strahlantenne f — omnidirectional antenna, omni antenna
~ strahlbetrieb m — omni operation

S

Sammel | anschluß m	PBX line group, hunt group
~ gesprächseinrichtung f	multi-party facility
~ ruf m	multi-address call
Satellit m	satellite
direktstrahlender ~	direct broadcasting satellite
geostationärer ~	geostationary satellite
Satelliten | amt n	satellite exchange
mobile ~ dienste mpl	mobile satellite services
~ -Erdefunkstelle f	satellite earth station
~ funk m, ~ kommunikation f	satellite communications
~ strecke f	satellite link
~ übertragung f	satellite transmission
Satz m (Verbindungssatz)	circuit
~ gruppe f	circuit group
Schalt | diversity f	switching diversity
~ kennzeichen n	switching signal
Schattenzone f	shadow zone, shaded area
Scheitelplatte f (Antenne f)	vertex plate
Schichten fpl	layers
Schicht 1: physikalische ~	physical layer
Schicht 2: Übertragungs- oder Datensicherungs ~	link layer
Schicht 3: Netzwerk- oder Vermittlungs ~	network layer
Schicht 4: Transport ~	transport layer
Schicht 5: Sitzungs ~	session layer
Schicht 6: Darstellungs ~	presentation layer
Schicht 7: Anwendungs ~	application layer
7-Schichtenmodell n	seven-layer model

Schichtenprotokoll n — layer protocol
Schirmzelle f — umbrella cell
schlechte Verständigung f — poor transmission
schlüsselfertiges System n — turnkey system
Schluß | kreuz n — end-of-selection (+), combination 26 (plus sign)
~ zeichen n — clearing signal, clearback signal
Schmal | banddienst m — narrowband service
~ bandkommunikation f — narrowband communications
~ bandkoppelnetz n — narrowband switching network
~ bandübertragung f — narrowband transmission
Schnittstelle f — interface
  gemeinsame Luft ~ — common air interface
  intelligente ~ — smart interface
  ~ für Paketvermittlungsnetze npl — interface for packet-switched networks
  Mobilstation-Basisstation- ~ — mobile-station-to-base-station interface
  Netz-Netz- ~ — internetwork interface
  Teilnehmer-Netz- ~ — user-network interface
  V-Serie-Schnittstellen fpl (für Datenübertragung f über Fernsprechwege mpl) — V-series interfaces
  X-Serie-Schnittstellen fpl (für Datenübertragung f in Datennetzen npl) — X-series interfaces
Schnittstellen | bedingungen fpl — interface specifications, interface requirements
~ norm f — interface standard
~ umsetzer m — interface converter
~ vervielfacher m — interface expander, interface multiplier
schnurlose Nebenstellenanlage f — cordless PABX, wireless PABX
~ s Telefon — cordless telephone
Schritt | dauer f — signal element length
~ geschwindigkeit f — modulation rate, signalling rate
Schutz | abstand m — protection ratio (against noise)
~ reserve f — protection margin
Schwebung f — beat

Schwellenüberschreitungszahl f	level crossing rate, LCR
schwinden	to fade (away)
Schwund m	fading
dispersiver ~	dispersive fading
frequenzselektiver ~	frequency-selective fading
langsamer ~	shadow fading, long-term fading, slow fading
selektiver ~	selective fading
Schwunddauer f	fading duration
schwundfrei	fading-free
Schwund | frequenz f	fading frequency
~ minderer m	anti-fading device
~ rate f	fading rate
Scrambler m	scrambler
See | funk m	marine radio
~ funkdienst m	ship-to-shore radio
beweglicher ~ funkdienst m	maritime mobile service
~ kabel n	submarine cable, undersea cable, ocean cable
segmentieren	to segment
Sektor | antenne f	sector antenna, sectorized antenna
~ betrieb m	sector operation
~ wiederholung f	sector reuse
~ zelle f	sector cell
Selbst | wählferndienstnetz n, öffentliches ~	public switched telephone network, PSTN
~ wählfernverkehr m	subscriber trunk dialling, STD, direct distance dialling, DDD
~ wählverbindung f	subscriber-dialled call
~ wählvermittlung f	automatic dial exchange
Selektiv | ruf m	selective call
~ schwund m	selective fading
Sende | abruf m	polling
~ antenne f	transmitter antenna, transmitting antenna
~ betrieb m	transmit mode, transmittal mode

~ -/Empfangseinrichtung f   transceiver, transmitter-receiver set
~ /Empfangseinrichtung f für den zentralen Zeichengabekanal m   signalling link transceiver
senden   to transmit
Sende | freigabesignal n   proceed-to-send signal
~ leistung f   output power, transmission power
~ leistungsanpassung f   adaptive power control
adaptive ~ leistungsregelung f   adaptive transmitter power control
~ leitung f   outgoing line, outgoing trunk
Sender m, Sendeeinrichtung f   transmitter
ortsfester ~   fixed transmitter
Sendeseite f   transmitting end
Server m   server
adaptierter ~   adapted server
~ -Zentralsteuerung f   server common control
Service 130   Service 130
Sicherheit f im Fernmeldeverkehr m   communications security, COMSEC
Sicherheitsdienst m   alarm service
sicherheitstechnische Software f   dependability system software
Sicherheitstechnik f   dependability system
Sicherungs | datenbank f, zentrale ~   central backup database
~ protokoll n   data link protocol, link access protocol
~ software f   dependability software
Sicht | ausbreitung f   line-of-sight propagation
~ linie f   line of sight
~ verbindung f   line-of-sight link
Signal n   signal
gewünschtes ~   wanted signal
ungewünschtes ~   unwanted signal
Signal-Geräuschabstand m   signal-to-noise ratio
Signalisierung f, Signalgabe f, (s. auch Zeichengabe)   signalling
Signal | laufzeit f   signal propagation time
~ -Nebensprechverhältnis n   signal-to-crosstalk ratio

~ pegel m	signal level
~ prozessor m	signal processor
~ -Rauschabstand m	signal-to-noise ratio, S/N ratio
~ -Störleistungsverhältnis n	signal-to-interference ratio, S/I ratio
~ umsetzer m, ~ wandler m	signal converter
~ unterdrückungsrauschen n	signal suppression noise
digitale ~ verarbeitung f	digital signal processing
~ verbindung f	link
~ wiederholung f	alarm repetition
Simplex, Wechselsprechen n	simplex
Sitzungsschicht f	session layer
~ -Verwaltung f	session layer management
skandinavisches Mobilfunksystem n	NMT (Nordic Mobile Telephone System)
Sofortverkehr m	demand traffic, demand service
Softtaste f	softkey
Software f	
ladbare ~	loadable software
sicherheitstechnische ~	dependability system software
vermittlungstechnische ~	call processing software
~ anbieter m (z.B. Btx)	software provider
Sonderdienst m	special service
spannungsempfindlich	voltage-sensitive
Speicher	betrieb m	store-and-forward mode
~ dienst m	store-and-forward service
speicherprogrammiert	stored-program . . .
~ e Wählvermittlung f	automatic stored-program switching center
Speicher	- und Verarbeitungsdienst m	store-and-forward service
~ verkehr m	delay call handling
~ vermittlung f	store-and-forward switching
~ vermittlungsstelle f	store-and-forward switching center
Spektralfrequenz f	spectral frequency
Sperre f	barring
abgehende ~	barring of all outgoing calls
abgehende internationale ~	barring of all outgoing international calls
ankommende ~	barring of all incoming calls

Sperreinrichtung f	barring facility
Sperren n von Anrufen mpl	call barring
~ eines Teilnehmers m	to busy out a subscriber
Sperr | funktion f	blocking function, inhibit function
~ signal n	blocking signal, inhibit signal
~ tabelle f	barring table
Spiegelfrequenz f	image frequency
Spitzen | belastung f	peak load
~ belastungszeit f	busy hours, peak hours
~ verkehr m	peak traffic
Sprach | band n (Frequenzen fpl)	voice band, speech band
~ box f	voice mailbox
~ dienst m	voice service
Sprache f	speech, voice
~ digitalisieren	to digitize speech
Sprach | frequenzbereich m	voice-frequency range
~ netz n	voice network
~ qualität f, erhöhte ~	enhanced voice quality
~ qualität f, hohe ~	high voice quality
~ speicherdienst m	message storage service, messenger service, voice storage and retrieval, voice mail box, voice mail service, voice-store-and-forward service
~ signal n	voice signal, speech signal
~ terminal n	voice terminal
~ übertragung f	speech transmission, voice transmission
~ - und Daten-Nebenstellenanlage f	voice/data PBX
~ - und Datennetz n	voice and data network
Einsatz m im ~ - und Datenverbund m	composite voice and data use
~ - und Datenvermittlung f	voice and data switching
sprachunterstützte Wahl f	audioscroll
Sprach | verarbeitung f	speech processing
~ verschleierung f	speech scrambling
~ verwürfler m	speech scrambler

Sprech | aktivitätserkennung f	voice activity detection, VAD
~ anlage f	intercom system, intercom
~ funk m, Funkfernsprechen n	radiotelephony
~ gebühren fpl, Funkkanal-gebühren fpl	toll charges, air-time charges
~ kanal m	voice channel
sprechkanalfrei	off-air
Sprech | kreis m	speech circuit
~ kreisprüfung f	cross office check
~ signal n	voice signal
~ taste f	push-to-talk button
~ zeit f	airtime
Spreizungscodierung f	interleaved coding
Stabantenne f	rod antenna
Standarddienst m	basic service, standard service
Standbildübertragung f	static-picture transmission
Stand | leitung f, festgeschaltete Leitung f	dedicated line
~ leitungskoppler m	switching matrix for dedicated lines
Standort m	site, location, position
~ aktualisierung f	location update
~ bereichskennung f	location area identification, LAI
~ bestimmung f, Ortung f	location tracking, position locating
~ datei f	location register, LR
~ diversity	site diversity, multiple-base-station diversity
automatische ~ erfassung f	location registration, self-location
~ informationen fpl	location information
~ kennung f	location identification
vorausgehende ~ klärung	site search
~ löschung f	location cancellation procedure, LCP
~ wahl f	siting
Start | -/Stopp-Verfahren n	start-stop system
~ -/Stopp-Verzerrung f	start-stop distortion

Statusabfrage f	status request
Steghohlleiter m	ridged waveguide
Stehbild n	still image
steil (Signal n)	steep-sloped
sternförmig verbinden	to connect radially
Stern | konfiguration f	star configuration
~ struktur f	star network
Steuer | kanal m,	control channel, (ISDN) D channel
festgeschalteter ~	dedicated control channel, DCCH
~ rechner m für Ver- mittlungssysteme npl	switching system processor
~ takt m	control clock pulse
Steuerung f,	control, controller
speicherprogrammierte ~	stored-program control
Steuerungsfreigabe f	control enable
stochastische Frequenzmodulation f	random frequency modulation
Stör | abstand m	signal-to-noise ratio, signal-to-interference ratio
~ abstrahlung f	interference radiated
~ einstrahlung f	interference received
~ feldstärke f	interference field strength, noise field strength
~ frequenz f	noise frequency
~ gebiet n, ~ bereich m	interference area
~ meldung f	alarm
~ muster n	interference pattern
~ pegel m	noise level
~ quelle f	interference source
~ signal n	interference signal, interfering signal
~ spektrum n	noise spectrum
Störung f	noise, interference, fault, failure
~ beseitigen	to clear a fault
~ durch Nachbarkanal m	adjacent-channel interference
künstliche ~ en fpl	man-made noise
naturgegebene (Funk-) ~	natural noise
störungs | arm	low-noise . . .
~ unempfindlich	fault-tolerant, noise-immune

Stör | wirkbreite f	failure penetration range
~zustand m	out-of-order condition
Stoß | betrieb m	peak traffic mode
~zeit f	peak traffic period, period of peak activity
Strahlauslenkung f	beam deflection
Strahlungsleistung f, äquivalente ~	effective radiated power
Strecken | abschnitt m	route section
~alarm m	route alarm
~dämpfung f	path loss, path attenuation
~kanal m	route channel
~takt m	route clock pulse
streifender Einfall m	grazing incidence
Streudämpfung f	spreading loss
Streuer m	scatterer
Streuung f	scattering
Stufen | profil n	step index profile
~profilfaser f	step index fiber, step index optical waveguide
suchen	to hunt
Suchen eines mobilen Anschlusses m	mobile access hunting
Such | stellung f	hunting position
~verfahren n für Leitungsbelegung f	line hunting method
~verfahren n mit Nullstellung f	search with homing
Summen | diversity	equal gain diversity
~häufigkeit f	cumulative distribution
Summer m	buzzer
synchron arbeiten	to work in synchronism
Synchronbetrieb m	synchronous mode
Synchronisationszeichen n	synchronizing signal
Synchronisierinformationen fpl	synchronization information
System | anschaltung f	system access
~ausfall m	system failure, system breakdown

~ dämpfung f total loss
~ hochlauf m system startup
~ merkmale npl system features
~ zugehörigkeit f system affiliation
~ zusammenbruch m system failure, system breakdown
~ zustandssteuerung f system status control

T

TACS (britisches Mobilfunksystem n) TACS (Total Access Communication System)

Takt m, Taktimpuls m clock, clock pulse
  netzinterner ~ internal network timing, internal network clock

Taktableitung f timing extraction

takten to clock, to time

taktgebunden adj clock-pulse-controlled, under clock control

  nicht ~ clock-independent

Takt | geber m clock generator
~ raster n timing pattern
~ - und Synchronisationsimpuls m clock and synchronizing pulse

Tandemzugriff m tandem access

Tarif m rate, tariff
~ zone f tariff zone

Tasten | fernsprecher m pushbutton (dialling) telephone
~ wahl f pushbutton dialling, pushbutton selection

Tast | pause f keying interval
~ wahlapparat m pushbutton phone, touch-tone set

TDMA-Zugriffsverfahren n	time division multiplex access
Teilbandcodierung f	subband coding
Teilnehmer m	subscriber, user, party, customer, station
~ besetzt	number busy
aktivierender ~	activating station
gerufener ~	called party, called subscriber
mobiler ~	mobile user, mobile subscriber
rufender ~	calling party, calling subscriber, caller
rufender ~ zahlt	calling party pays, CPP
stationärer ~	stationary user
~ am zellularen Mobilfunk m	cellular subscriber
~ mit tragbarem Mobiltelefon n	portable subscriber
Teilnehmer | anschluß m	subscriber line
~ apparat m	subscriber set
~ autorisierungsschlüssel m	subscriber authentication key
~ betriebsklasse f	class of service, user class of service
~ datei f, Aufenthaltsdatei f	location register
~ daten pl	subscriber data, subscriber information
~ datenbank f	subscriber database
~ gerät n	subscriber unit
~ geräte npl	subscriber equipment, user equipment
geschlossene ~ gruppe f	closed user group, CUG
~ kapazität f	subscriber capacity
~ kennung f	subscriber identification, network user identifier, NUI
zeitweilige ~ kennung	temporary mobile subscriber identity, TMSI
~ kennungsmodul n	subscriber identity module, SIM
~ klasse	subscriber class
~ kreis m	subscriber base
~ nutzungsverhalten n	subscriber usage pattern
~ -Teilnehmer-Zeichengabe f	user-to-user signalling, UUS
~ verhalten n	subscriber behaviour
~ verzeichnis n	directory of subscribers, user directory
bedienbare ~ zahl f	customer handling capacity
Teil | strecke f	link
~ welle f	component wave
Telebox f	mailbox
Teledienste mpl	teleservices

Telefaxdienst	facsimile transmission service
Telefonbuch n, elektronisches ~	electronic telephone directory
Telefon-Konferenz f, Konferenzgespräch n	conference calling, telephone conference
Telegrafie f, drahtlose ~	radio telegraphy
Telematik f	telematics
Telemetrie f	telemetry, telemetering
Teletex, Tex	teletex
~ dienst m	teletex service
~ -Endgerät n	teletex terminal, teletex station
~ netz n	teletex network
~ teilnehmer m	teletex subscriber
Telex, Tx	telex
~ -Anschaltgerät n	telex terminal repeater
~ fernschaltgerät n	telex signalling unit
~ netz n	telex network
~ teilnehmer m	telex subscriber, telex terminal
TEMEX (Fernwirk-, Fernmeß- und Fernüberwachungsdienst)	telemetry exchange
Terminal n, Endgerät n	terminal
Terminspeicher m	appointment storage
Test | mobil n	test mobile
~ protokoll n	test log
~ tonreferenz f	test tone reference
textbegleitende Sprechverbindung f	speech connection with accompanying text transmission
Tiefpaßfilterung f	low-pass filtering
Tiefschwund m	deep fade
Tisch | apparat m	table telephone
~ fernkopierer m	desktop facsimile equipment, tabletop facsimile equipment
Token | -Passing-Zugang m	token-passing access
~ -Ring m (Netz n)	token ring
Ton m, einen ~ anlegen	to inject a tone

Ton | ausbreitungsweg m — audio path
~ frequenzwahl f — voice-frequency signalling, VF signalling
~ -plus-Stimme-Funkrufdienst m — tone plus voice paging
~ qualität f — tone quality
~ signal n — tone signal
~ wahl f — voice-frequency signalling

Topologie f — topology

Totalschwund m — fade-out

Träger | dienst m (ISDN) — bearer service
~ frequenz f — carrier frequency
~ frequenzversatz m — carrier frequency offset
~ kanal m — carrier channel, (ISDN) bearer channel
~ leitung f — carrier circuit, carrier line
~ -Rauschabstand m, ~ -Rauschleistungsverhältnis n — carrier-to-noise ratio, C/N ratio
~ -Störleistungsverhältnis n (Verhältnis n zwischen gewünschtem und ungewünschtem Signal n) — carrier-to-interference ratio, C/I ratio, CIR
~ stromverstärker m — carrier repeater
~ welle f — carrier wave

Transfer | geschwindigkeit f — data transfer rate
übergreifende ~ zeit f — cross-office transfer time

Transit | knoten m — transit node, intermediate node
~ verbindung f — transit call
~ verkehr m — transit traffic
~ vermittlung f — transit exchange, tandem switching
Breitband- ~ vermittlung f — broadband transit exchange

Transparent-Modus m — transparent mode

Transponder f — transponder

Transportschicht f — transport layer

Trennanforderung f — disconnect request

trennen (Anruf) — to disconnect (call)

Trennschärfe f, Selektivität f — selectivity
~ gegen den Nachbarkanal m — adjacent-channel selectivity

Trichterstrahler m — horn radiator

Tür | freisprecheinrichtung f entrance telephone system
~ freisprechstelle f entrance telephone
Turmantenne f tower antenna

U

Über | belegung f congestion
~ dimensionierung f overdimensioning
~ gabebestätigung f delivery confirmation
übergeordnetes Amt n higher-ranking exchange
überkanalisieren to over-channelize
überlagerte Funkzone f overlaid cell
Überlagerungsempfang m heterodyne reception
Überland-. . . cross-country . . .
Über | lastung f overload, congestion, route congestion
~ leiteinrichtung f, Mobilvermittlungsstelle f, Funkvermittlungseinrichtung f mobile services switching center, mobile switching center, MSC
~ mittlungsabschnitt m transmission section, data link
~ mittlungsdienst m bearer service, transmission service
~ mittlungsgeschwindigkeit f data rate
~ reichweitenstörung f overreach interference
~ sprechdämpfung f crosstalk attenuation
~ sprechen, Nebensprechen n crosstalk
übertragen, digital ~ to transmit digitally
Übertragung f transmission
  abschnittsweise ~ section-by-section transmission
  analoge ~ analog transmission
  asynchrone ~ asynchronous transmission

digitale ~	digital transmission
drahtlose ~	radio transmission
envelopeweise ~	envelope-mode transmission
serielle ~	serial transmission
simultane ~	simultaneous transmission
synchrone ~	synchronous transmission
versuchte ~	attempted transmission
Übertragungs | dämpfung f	transmission loss
~ geschwindigkeit f	signalling speed (bits/s)
~ güte f, ~ qualität f	transmission quality
~ leistung f	transmission performance
~ schicht f	link layer
~ sicherheit f	transmission reliability
~ strecke f	transmission link
~ wagen m	mobile transmitter
~ weg m	transmission path
Überwachungston m	supervisory tone
Umbuch | antrag m	cell change request
~ nachricht f	roaming indication, updating request
umcodieren, gleichstromfrei ~	to convert (signals) with no dc component
Umlaufbahn f (Satellit m)	orbit
geostationäre ~	geostationary orbit
umleiten, umsteuern	to re-route, to divert
Umleitung f	diverse routing, rerouting, redirection
Umlenkung f	route diversion
umpolen	to reverse polarity
Umschalttaste f	shift key
Umstecken n am Bus m	bus changeover
Umtastung f (Modulation f digitaler Signale npl)	shift keying
Umweg m	alternate route
~ lenkung f	alternate routing
~ signal n	multipath signal
unabhängig, nicht angeschlossen	off-line
unbedient	unattended, unmanned

unbedingte Anrufumlenkung f	call forwarding unconditional
unerwünschte Aussendungen fpl	unwanted emissions
ungewünschtes Signal n	unwanted signal
Unterband n	lower half band
unterbrochene Verbindung f	disrupted connection
untergebracht: im selben Raum m / Gebäude n etc. ~	co-located
Unterdrückung f der Anzeige f der Nummer f des gerufenen Teilnehmers m	connected line identification restriction
~ der Anzeige f der Nummer f des rufenden Teilnehmers m	calling line identification restriction
Unterkanal m	subchannel
unterlagerte Funkzone f	underlaid cell
unterstützen (z.B. ein Verfahren n)	to support (a procedure)
unvollendete Verbindung f	incomplete connection
Ursprungs | amt n, Ursprungs-vermittlungsstelle f	originating exchange
~ bündel n	originating trunk group

Validierung f	validation
Verarbeitungsrechner m	host, host computer
verbinden, durchverbinden	to connect through
~ wenn frei	connect-when-free facility
Verbindung f	call, connection, circuit
abgehende ~	mobile-to-land call, outgoing call

Verbindung — Verbindungswunsch

ankommende ~	land-to-mobile call, incoming call
direkt durchgeschaltete ~	direct station-to-station connection
feste virtuelle ~	permanent virtual circuit
geparkte ~	parked call
gewählte virtuelle ~	switched virtual circuit
~ hergestellt	connected
eine ~ herstellen	to establish a connection, to set up a call
nicht zugelassene ~	inadmissible call
nicht zustandegekommene ~	uncompleted call, ineffective call
platzvermittelte ~	operator-assisted call, operator-initiated call
unterbrochene ~	disrupted connection
unvollendete ~	incomplete connection
wegen Besetztseins nicht zustandegekommene ~	uncompleted call due to busy condition
zurückgewiesene ~	lost call
zustandegekommene ~	completed call, effective call

Verbindungs | abbau m — connection cleardown
~ anforderung f — call request
~ aufbau m — call establishment, call set-up
~ aufbau m ohne Sprechkanalbelegung f, sprechkanalfreier ~ aufbau m — off-air call setup, OACSU
selbsttätiger ~ aufbau m — hot-line service
~ aufbaurichtung f — connection setup direction
~ aufrechterhaltung f — call maintenance
~ bearbeitung f — call handling, call processing
~ dauer f — call duration
gebührenpflichtige ~ dauer f — chargeable call duration
mittlere ~ dauer f — average call duration
~ häufigkeit f — calling rate
~ herstellzeit f — setup time, connecting delay
~ übergabe f, Gesprächsumschaltung f — handoff
~ überwachung f — call supervision, connection monitoring
~ versuch m — call attempt
wiederholter ~ versuch m — repeated call attempt
~ wunsch m — call request, call intent

~ zusammenstoß m	call collision, head-on collision
~ zustandsdaten pl	connection status data
verbunden: falsch ~	wrong number
Verbunden-Signal n	call-connected signal, ringback signal
Verbundnetz n	integrated network, mixed network
Verfolgung f, elektronische ~	computerized tracking
Verfolgungssystem n	tracking system
Verfügbarkeitsdauer f mittlere ~ zwischen zwei Ausfällen mpl, mittlere Ausfallabstand m	mean time between failures, MTBF
Verkehr m	traffic
abgehender ~ , gehender ~	outgoing traffic, outbound traffic
ankommender ~ , kommender ~	incoming traffic, inbound traffic
Verkehr m abwickeln	to handle traffic
Verkehrs | angebot n	offered traffic
~ aufkommen n	traffic volume, traffic demand
räumliches ~ aufkommen n	spatial traffic demand
~ aufteilung f	traffic distribution
~ auswertung f	traffic analysis
mittlere ~ belastung f	mean traffic load, mean traffic carried
~ dichte f	traffic density
~ güte f	quality of service, grade of service
~ kanal m	traffic channel, TCH
~ kapazität f	traffic handling capacity
~ last f	traffic load
~ leistung f	traffic carrying capacity
~ lenkung f	routing
adaptive ~ lenkung f	adaptive routing
feste ~ lenkung f	fixed routing
~ modell n	traffic model
~ simulation f	traffic simulation
~ spitze f	traffic peak
~ stauung f	traffic congestion
~ verhalten n, ~ verlauf m	traffic pattern
~ verteilung f	traffic distribution
~ zählung f	traffic count
~ zunahme f	traffic growth

verlustarm	low-loss . . .
Verlustbelegung f	lost call
verlustlos	loss-free
Verlustwahrscheinlichkeit f	loss probability, lost call probability, probability of loss
Vermaschung f	redundant routing
vermieten (Leitungen fpl)	to lease
vermitteln	to switch
Vermittlung f (Vorgang)	switching
(Amt)	exchange
Vermittlungs | güte f	grade of switching performance
~ knoten m	switching node
~ leistung f	call processing rate
~ protokoll n	network protocol
~ rechner m	switching processor
~ schicht f	network layer
~ stelle f	exchange, exchange center, switch
analoge ~ stelle f	analog exchange
digitale ~ stelle f	digital switch
rechnergesteuerte ~ stelle f	computer-controlled exchange
speicherprogrammierte elektronische ~ stelle f	stored-program electronic switch
vermittlungstechnische Daten f	overhead data
~ Peripherie f	switching-oriented periphery, call processing periphery
~ Software f	call processing software
Vernetzung f	networking
Verrechnungsstelle f	clearing house
Versatzkanal m	interleaved channel
versorgen	to serve, to provide coverage (e.g. to a cell)
Versorger m, bester ~	best server
Versorgung f	coverage
flächendeckende ~	full coverage
landesweite ~	nationwide coverage
~ der Bevölkerung f	population coverage

~ mit tragbaren Funktelefonen npl	portable coverage
~ mit dem Zellularsystem n	cellular coverage
Versorgungs | bereich m, ~ gebiet n	coverage area, service area
sich überlappende ~ gebiete npl	coverage overlap
~ grad m	coverage rate
~ lücke f	coverage gap
~ wahrscheinlichkeit f	coverage probability, service probability
Verständigungsverkehr m	voice coordination traffic
Verstärker m	repeater, enhancer, amplifier
C-Verstärker m	class-C amplifier
Verstärkungsregelung f	gain control
verstümmelt	mutilated, garbled
Versuch m, erfolgloser ~	unsuccessfull (call) attempt
Versuchsstrecke f	test route
verteilen (Frequenz f)	to allot
Verteilung f, kumulative ~, Summenhäufigkeit f	cumulative distribution
Verträglichkeitsmatrix f	compatibility matrix
verwerfen	to ignore, to discard
Verwürfelung f	scrambling
Verwürfler m	scrambler
Verzerrung f	distortion
Verzögerungs | -Doppler-Spektrum n	delay-Doppler spectrum
~ -Leistungsspektrum n	delay power spectrum, power delay profile
~ zeit f	delay time
Verzonung f	zoning
Videokonferenz f	videoconference
Videotex (internationale Bezeichnung für Bildschirmtext ,,Btx'')	videotex
Videotext m (für Empfang über Farbfernsehgerät)	videotext

Vielfach | zugriff m im Codemultiplex n, Vielfachzugriff m durch Codemodulation f	code division multiple access, CDMA
~ zugriff m im Frequenzmultiplex n, Mehrfachzugriff m durch Frequenzaufteilung f	frequency division multiple access
~ zugriff m im Zeitmultiplex n, Zeitmultiplex-Vielfachzugriff m	time division multiple access, TDMA
~ -Zugriffsverfahren	multiplex access
Vielsprecher m	high-calling-rate subscriber
Vier | bandvertauschung f	four-band inversion
~ drahtleitung f	four-wire line
~ phasenumtastung f	quadrature phase shift keying, QPSK
virtuelle Verbindung f	virtual circuit
volldigital	all-digital . . .
Vollzugsordnung f für den Funkdienst m	Radio Regulations, RR
Vorbestellung f (von Verbindungen fpl)	advance booking
Vorortsverkehr m	suburban traffic
Vorrangverbindung f	priority call, priority connection
Vorrechner m	front-end processor
Vorwahlkennziffer f	prefix number
V.24-Schnittstelle f	V.24-interface

W

Wähl | betrieb m	dial operation
automatische ~ einrichtung f	automatic call unit
(im Datenverkehr m)	
wählen (Tastatur)	to select
(Wählscheibe)	to dial
Wähl | scheibe f	dial
Telefon mit ~ tastatur f	pushbutton set
~ ton m	dial tone
~ verbindung f	dialling line, switched connection, dial connection
~ verkehr m	dialled traffic
speicherprogrammierte	automatic stored-program switching
~ vermittlung	center
Wahl f bei aufliegendem Hörer m	on-hook dialling
abgesetzte ~	interrupted dialling
Wahl | aufforderungszeichen n,	proceed-to-select signal,
~ bereitzeichen n	start-dialling signal
~ code m abfragebereit	selection code presented
~ informationen fpl	dialling information
~ wiederholung f	automatic redial(ling), last number redialing, number redial feature
~ wiederholung wenn gerufener Anschluß m belegt	completion of calls to busy subscribers
WAN (wide area network)	WAN (großflächiges Kommunikationsnetz)
Wandern n, Roaming	roaming

Wartedauer f	delay
mittlere ~ aller Belegungen fpl	mean delay of all calls
mittlere ~ der wartenden Belegungen fpl	mean delay of calls delayed
Warte	schlange f	queue, waiting queue
~ schlangenbetrieb m	queuing, call queuing, call holding operation
~ stellung f	queuing condition
in ~ stellung f schalten	to camp on busy, to camp a call onto a trunk
~ system n	queuing system
~ verkehr m	queuing operation, call holding operation
~ wahrscheinlichkeit f	queuing probability
Wechselsprechen n, Simplex n	simplex
Wecker m, Klingel f	prompter, bell, ringer
weiterleiten	to route, to forward
Weiterleitung f	forwarding
Weiter	reichanforderung f	handover request
~ reichen n	handover
~ reichen n der Verbindung f	intercell handoff
~ reichkriterium n	handover criterion
~ reichstrategie f	handover strategy
~ reichvorgang m	handover event, hand-off
Durchführung f des ~ reichvorgangs m	handover execution
nicht zustandegekommener ~ reichvorang m	missed handover
Wellen	ausbreitung f	wave propagation
~ längenmultiplexer m	wave length multiplexer
~ längenbereich m	band
~ leiter m	waveguide
Welt	datenwählnetz n	worldwide switched data network
~ funkverwaltungskonferenz f	World Administrative Radio Conference, WARC
~ kommunikationsnetz n	global area network, worldwide communications network
~ münzer m, ~ münzfernsprecher m	worldwide pay phone

weltweite Funkverwaltungskonferenz f für Mobilfunk m	world administrative radio conference for mobile services, WARC-MOB
~ Funkverwaltungskonferenz f für Satelliten-Dienste mpl	world administrative radio conference for orbital services, WARC-ORB
Wenigsprecher m	low-calling-rate subscriber
Wieder | aufnahme f der Verbindung f	call reestablishment
~ einschaltversuch m	restoral attempt
~ herstellung f	recovery, restoration
~ holabstand m	reuse distance
wiederholter Versuch m	retry
Wieder | holung f	reuse, retry
automatische ~ holungssanforderung f	automatic request for repeat
~ inbetriebnahme f	return to service
Winkeldiversity	angle diversity, direction diversity
Wortfehlerquote f	word error rate

X.25-Protokoll n	X.25 protocol
x/y-Schnittstelle f	x/y interface

Z

Zähltakt m	counting pulse
Zeichen | abgabeverkehr m	interexchange information
~ anforderung f	character request
~ fehlerwahrscheinlichkeit f	character error probability
~ gabe f, Signalisierung f	signalling
abschnittsweise ~ gabe f	link-by-link signalling
assoziierte ~ gabe f	associated signalling
kanalgebundene ~ gabe f	channel-associated signalling
Mehrfrequenz ~ gabe f	multi-frequency signalling
Teilnehmer-Teilnehmer ~ gabe	user-to-user signalling, UUS
~ gabe f im Verbindungszustand m	in-service control signalling
~ gabe f mit gemeinsamem Zeichenkanal m	common channel signalling
~ gabeabschnitt m	signalling link
~ gabebits npl	Sn bits
~ gabeinformationen fpl	signalling information
~ gabekanal m	signalling channel
zentraler ~ gabekanal m	common signalling channel
~ gabeprotokoll n	signalling protocol
~ gabesystem n Nr. 7	signalling system No. 7 (SS #7)
~ gabeverkehr m	signalling traffic
Zeichen geben	to signal
Zeichen | puffer m	signal buffer
~ satz m	character set, character repertoire
~ takt m	character timing
Zeitbereichsentzerrer m, adaptiver ~	adaptive time domain equalizer
Zeitdiversity	time diversity
Zeiten fpl niedriger Verkehrsbelastung f	non-busy hours, off-peak hours

Zeit | multiplexbetrieb m, im ~ arbeiten   to operate in a time-division mode
~ multiplex-Durchschaltenetz n   time-division multiplex network
~ multiplexverfahren n   time division multiplexing
~ multiplex-Vielfachzugriff m   time division multiple access, TDMA
~ raster m   time-slot pattern
~ schlitz m, ~ intervall n   time slot
aktiver Teil m des ~ es   active part of time slot
~ schlitzeinblendung f   blank-burst mode
~ skala f   time frame
~ taktimpuls m   time pulse
~ zählung f   time metering
~ zonenzähler m   time and zone meter, time and distance meter

Zellbündel n   cluster

Zelle f mit Rundstrahlantenne f   omni cell

Zellenstation f   cell site

Zellteilung f   cell splitting

Zellulardienste mpl   cellular services

zellulare Netzstruktur f   cellular network structure
~ s Funknetz n   cellular radio network
~ s Funksystem n   cellular radio system
~ r Mobilfunk m   cellular mobile radio
~ r Telefondienst m   cellular phone service

Zellular | netz n, digitales ~   digital cellular network
~ system n   cellular system
~ telefonie f, Zellenfunktelefonie f   cellular radio telephony, cellular telephony, cellular radio

zentraler Zeichengabekanal m   common signalling channel

Zentralkanal-Zeichengabe f   common channel signalling
~ - ~ verfahren Nr. 7   common channel signalling system # 7 (CCITT)

Zentral | prozessor m   co-ordination processor
~ vermittlungsstelle f   central switch
~ vermittlungsstellenbereich m   tertiary area

Zielamt n   destination exchange

Zielwahl f mit Namentasten fpl	speed calling with name keys
Zone f	zone, cell
versorgende ~	serving cell
tote ~	zone of silence, silent zone
Zonen | gebühr f	zone rate
~ sektorierung f	cell sectorization
Zubringer | bündel n	offering trunk group
~ leitung f	offering trunk
Zugang m	access
verschlüsselter ~	encrypted access
vorrangiger ~	priority access
Zugangs | anforderung f	access request
~ art f	category of access
~ bewilligung f	access grant
~ burst n	access burst, AB
~ gebühr f	access charge
~ kennzahl f	access code
internationale ~ kennzahl f	international prefix
~ konflikt m	access contention
~ pfad m	link
~ protokoll n	access protocol
~ prozedur f	access procedure
~ punkt m	port
~ weg m	access link
Zug | funk m	train radio
~ telefon n	train telephone
Zugriffs | kanal m	access channel
~ verfahren n	access mode
Zulässigkeitsprüfung f	barring check
Zuordnungswahrscheinlichkeit f	assignment probability
zurückrufen	to call back, to ring back
Zusammen | schaltung f	interconnection
~ stoß m	collision
~ treffen n von Mikrowellen fpl auf halbem Weg m	mid-air meeting of microwaves
Zusatz | dämpfung f	excess path loss
~ dienste mpl	enhanced services, supplementary services

~ dienstmerkmale npl — enhanced service features
Zustandsabfragesignal n — status inquiry signal
Zustimmmung f zur Gebührenübernahme f — reverse charging acceptance
zuteilen (Frequenz f) — to assign
Zuverlässigkeit f der Zeichengabe f — signalling reliability
Zuverlässigkeits- und Ausfallanalyse f — reliability and failure analysis
zuweisen (Frequenz f) — to allocate
Zwangsumschaltung f — forced handoff
Zweidrahtleitung f — two-wire line
Zweieranschluß m — two-party line
Zweigamt n — branch exchange
Zweiphasenumtastung f, 2-PSK — binary phase shift keying, BPSK
Zweitweg m — secondary route
Zwischen | knoten m — transit node
~ knotenleitung f — inter-nodal line
~ leitung f — link
~ meldung f — progress message
zwischenspeichern — to buffer
Zyklusanforderung f — cycle request
Zylinderbeugungsdämpfung f — cylindrical diffraction

Englisch-Deutsch

A

abandoned call	abgebrochener Anruf
abbreviated dial code	Kurzwahlzeichen
~ dialling	Kurzwahl
~ directory number	Kurzwahlzeichen
abort vb (program)	abbrechen, verlassen
absent subscriber service	Fernsprechauftragsdienst
acceptance	Akzeptanz
access vb	sich anschalten
access	Zugang, Zugriff
~ barred signal	Antwortkennzeichen "Zugang verhindert"
~ burst	Zugangsburst
~ card	Berechtigungskarte
~ channel	Zugriffskanal
~ charge	Zugangsgebühr
~ code	Zugangskennzahl
~ grant	Zugangsbewilligung
~ hunting, mobile ~	Anrufverteilung
~ible adj	benutzbar, zugänglich
~ line	Anschlußleitung
~ link	Zugangsweg
~ mode	Zugangsverfahren
~ procedure	Zugangsprozedur
~ protocol	Zugangsprotokoll
~ request	Zugangsanforderung
encrypted ~	verschlüsselter Zugang
priority ~	vorrangiger Zugang
acknowledge vb	quittieren

acknowledge message	Rückmeldung
~ signal	Quittungssignal
~d interaction	Dialog mit Quittierung
~ ment	Quittierung, Quittung, Quittungsaustausch, Quittungsbetrieb, Rückmeldung
~ enable signal	Quittungsfreigabe
~ priority	Rückmeldepriorität
~ to originator	Quittierungsgabe zum Absender
negative ~, NAK	negative Quittierung
positive ~, ACK	positive Quittierung
acoustic call waiting, acoustic camp-on	akustisches Anklopfen
~ coupler	Akustikkoppler
activate vb	ansteuern, bereitstellen, (Mobilstation) einschalten
activating station	aktivierender Teilnehmer
activation	Anmeldung, Bereitstellung
~ charge	Anschlußgebühr
non-recurring ~ charge	einmalige Bereitstellungsgebühr
active subscribers file	Aktivdatei
~ part of time slot	aktiver Teil des Zeitintervalles
actuate vb	betätigen, drücken (Taste)
adaptation	Anpassung
adapted server	adaptierter Server
adaptive equalization	adaptive Entzerrung
~ frame alignment	adaptive Rahmensynchronisierung
~ power control	Sendeleistungsanpassung
~ routing	adaptive Verkehrslenkung
~ time domain equalizer	adaptiver Zeitbereichsentzerrer
~ transmitter power control	adaptive Sendeleistungsregelung
added-feature telephone	Komforttelefon
address call	Adressenaufruf
adjacent adj	benachbart
~ area	Nachbarbereich
~ base station	Nachbarfunkfeststation, benachbarte Basisstation

~ cell	Nachbarfunkzone, Nachbarzelle
~ channel	benachbarter Kanal, Nachbarkanal
~-channel attenuation	Nachbarkanaldämpfung
~-channel interference	Störung durch den Nachbarkanal, Nachbarkanalstörung
~-channel selectivity	Trennschärfe gegen den Nachbarkanal, Nachbarkanalselektivität
~ exchange	Nachbaramt
~ radio zone	benachbarte Funkzone
administration and data server	Betriebs- und Datenserver
~ and maintenance organization	betriebstechnische Organisation
~, maintenance and dependability integration	betriebs- und sicherungstechnische Integration
advance booking	Vorbestellung (von Verbindungen)
advice of charge, AOC	Gebührenanzeige
AF protection ratio, audio-frequency protection ratio	NF-Schutzabstand
~ signal-to-interference ratio	NF-Störabstand
air, off the air	außer Betrieb (Sender)
on the air	in Betrieb (Sender)
~ interface	Luftschnittstelle
common ~ interface	gemeinsame Luftschnittstelle
airfone	öffentlicher Telefonanschluß im Flugzeug
airtime	Gesprächszeit, Sprechzeit
~ charges	Funkkanalgebühren, Sprechgebühren
~ reseller	Wiederverkäufer von Gesprächszeit, Diensteanbieter
alarm	Störmeldung
~ and emergency services	Alarm- und Notrufdienste
~ condition monitoring	Alarmzustandsüberwachung
~ handling, ~ processing	Alarmbehandlung
~ interrupt request	Alarmunterbrechungsanforderung
~ repetition	Signalwiederholung
~ service	Sicherheitsdienst
~ signalling frame	Gruppensignalrahmen
major ~	dringender Alarm
alerting tone	Hinweiston

all-digital . . .	volldigital
all-glass fiber	Ganzglasfaser (Lichtwellenleiter)
allocate vb (frequencies)	(Frequenzen) zuweisen
allot vb (frequencies)	(Frequenzen) verteilen
all trunks busy	äußere Blockierung
all-trunks-busy time	Blockierungsdauer
alpha mode	Alpha-Betriebsweise (ISDN)
alphanumeric paging	alphanumerischer Funkrufdienst
alternate mark inversion code	AMI-Code, alternierendes Flanken-Pulsverfahren
~ route	Ausweichleitweg, Ersatzweg, Umweg
~ routing	Umweglenkung
~ trunk group	Ausweichbündel
alternating between call keys	Makeln zwischen Abfrageorganen
alternative channel	Ersatzkanal
amplifier	Verstärker
class-C ~	C-Verstärker
amplitude distortion	Amplitudenverzerrung
~ modulation, AM	amplitude modulation, AM
~ shift keying, ASK	Amplitudenumtastung
analog exchange	analoge Vermittlungsstelle
~ network	Analognetz
~ telephone	Analogtelefon
~ telephone network	analoges Fernsprechnetz
~ -to-digital converter,	A/D-Wandler, Analog-Digital-Wandler
~ -digital converter, A-D converter	
~ transmission	analoge Übertragung
analyze vb (service signals)	auswerten (z.B. Dienstsignale), bewerten
angle diversity	Winkeldiversity
~ of reflection	Reflexionswinkel (Lichtwellenleiter)
announcement	Ansage
answer vb	abarbeiten (Rufe), beantworten (Anrufe), abfragen, melden

~ a call	einen Anruf entgegennehmen
~ a page	einen Funkruf beantworten
answerback exchange	Kennungsaustausch, Kennungstausch
~ verification	Kennungsprüfung
answering	Melden
~ and monitoring machine	Abfrage- und Mitlesemaschine
~ circuit	Abfrageschaltung
~ delay	Meldeverzug
~ station	Gegenfunkstelle
~ tone	Antwortton
answerphone	Anrufbeantworter
answer pulse	Meldeimpuls
~ signal	Meldesignal
antenna, aerial	Antenne
~ area	Antennenausleuchtungsgebiet
~ bearing	Antennenrichtung
~ coverage	Antennenausleuchtungsgebiet
~ diversity	Antennendiversity
~ gain	Antennengewinn
~ height, effective ~	wirksame Antennenhöhe
~ location	Antennenstandort
~ mast	Antennenmast
~ multiplexer	Antennenkoppler
~ multiplexing	Antennenmehrfachausnutzung
~ orientation	Antennenausrichtung
~ site	Antennenstandort
~-switched diversity	Antennenschaltdiversity
~ tower	Antennenturm
down-tilted ~	nach unten neigende Antenne
isotropic ~	isotrope Antenne
omni-directional ~	rundstrahlende Antenne
receiving ~	Empfangsantenne
retracted ~	eingefahrene Antenne
tiltable ~	umlegbare Antenne
top-loaded ~	oben beschwerte Antenne
anti-fading device	Schwundminderer
application layer	Anwendungsschicht
~ protocol	Anwendungsprotokoll (ISDN)

appointment storage	Terminspeicher
area code	Bereichskennzahl, Ortsnetzkennzahl, Funkbereichskennzahl
~ coverage	Gebietsüberdeckung
~ mean	Langstreckenmittelwert
~ of industrial concentration	Ballungsgebiet (Gewerbe und Industrie)
~-to-area model	Flächenmodell
built-up ~ s	bebaute Gebiete
developed ~ s	erschlossene Gebiete
open ~ s	offenes Gelände
outlying ~ s	abgelegene Gebiete
rural ~ s	ländliche Gebiete
urban ~	städtische Gebiete, urbane Gebiete
architecture model	Architekturmodell
ascending (traffic)	aufsteigend
ASCII (American Standard Code for Information Interchange)	genormter Code für Nachrichtenaustausch
assign vb (frequencies)	(Frequenzen) zuteilen
assignment probability	Zuordnungswahrscheinlichkeit
associated signalling	assoziierte Zeichengabe
asynchronous mode	Asynchronbetrieb
~ /synchronous converter	Asynchron-/Synchron-Umsetzer
~ transmission	asynchrone Übertragung
attempt, unsuccessful (call) ~	erfolgloser Versuch
~ ed transmission	versuchte Übertragung
~ to occupy mobile stations	Belegungsversuch
attended exchange	bemanntes Amt
~ operation	bedienter Betrieb
attenuate vb	dämpfen (z.B. Signal)
attenuation (dB)	Dämpfung, Leistungsabfall, Leistungsverlust (in dB)
attrition rate (of customers/subscribers)	Fluktuationsrate
audible busy signal	akustisches Besetztzeichen

audioconference	Audiokonferenz
audio path	Tonausbreitungsweg
audioscroll	sprachunterstützte Wahl
audio tone frequency shift modulated carrier	FSK-Träger
authenticate vb	autorisieren
authorization	Berechtigung
personal ~	personenbezogene Berechtigung
autocorrelation function	Autokorrelationsfunktion, AKF
automatic analog public telephone network	öffentliches analoges Fernsprechwählnetz
~ call unit	automatische Wähleinrichtung (im Datenverkehr)
~ dial exchange	Selbstwählvermittlung
~ call distributor	automatischer Anrufverteiler
~ call maker	automatisches Anrufgerät
~ handoff	Gesprächsweiterleitung (bei Funkzonenwechsel)
~ redial(ling)	Wahlwiederholung
~ repeat request, ARQ	automatische Fehlerkorrektur durch Rückfrage
~ stored-program switching center	speicherprogrammierte Wählvermittlungsstelle
automobile telephone service	Autotelefondienst
~ telephone subscriber	Autotelefon-Teilnehmer
autotracking	Eigennachführung
availability	Erreichbarkeit, Verfügbarkeit
constant ~	konstante Verfügbarkeit
full ~	volle Verfügbarkeit
limited ~	begrenzte Verfügbarkeit
average call duration	mittlere Verbindungsdauer

B

backbone network	Backbone-Netz (zur Verbindung inkompatibler Netze), Hintergrundnetz
background test	Hintergrundtest
backing up	Datensicherung
back-to-back connected	antiparallelgeschaltet
backup database, central ~ database	zentrale Sicherungsdatenbank
~ mode	Reservebetrieb
~ system	Ersatzanlage
backward channel	Hilfskanal, Rückkanal
band	Band, Wellenlängenbereich
bandfilter	Bandfilter
band inversion	Bandinvertierung
bandpass	Bandpaß
~ filter	Bandfilter
bandwidth	Bandbreite
correlation ~	Korrelationsbandbreite
barring	Sperre
~ check	Zulässigkeitsprüfung
~ facility	Sperreinrichtung
~ of all incoming calls	ankommende Sperre
~ of all outgoing calls	abgehende Sperre
~ of all outgoing international calls	abgehende internationale Sperre
~ table	Sperrtabelle
call ~	Sperren von Anrufen
base	Basis
~ processor	Basisprozessor

~ station	Basisstation, Funkfeststation, ortsfeste Landfunkstelle,
~ station area	Einzugsbereich (der Basisstation), Basisstationsbereich
~ station code	Kennung der Basisstation
~ station controller, BSC	Basisstationssteuerung
~ station identity code, BSIC	Kennung der Basisstation
~ station interface, BSI	Basisstationsschnittstelle
low-power ~ station	Kleinleistungs-Basisstation
serving ~ station	betreuende Basisstation, versorgende Basisstation
baseband	Basisband
~ equipment	Basisbandgerät
~ frequency	Basisbandfrequenz
base-to-mobile	ankommend
basic access	Basisanschluß (Netz), Basiskanal
~ clock rate	Grundtakt
~ interface multiplexer	Basisanschluß-Multiplexer
~ propagation loss	Grundübertragungsdämpfung
~ pulse rate	Grundtakt
~ service attribute	Basisdienstmerkmal
~ services	Grunddienste, Standarddienste
~ transmission loss	Grundübertragungsdämpfung
baud, bd	Baud, Bd
Baudot code (five-channel code)	Baudot-Code (Fernschreiber)
B channel	B-Kanal (Nutz- oder Basiskanal im ISDN)
BCH (Bose-Chauduri-Hocquenghem) code	BCH-Code
beam deflection	Strahlauslenkung
bearer services	Bearer Services, Trägerdienste, Übermittlungsdienste (im ISDN)
~ channel	Trägerkanal
bearing indication	Peilanzeige
beat	Schwebung
beep	Piepston

bell	Klingel, Wecker
best server	bester Versorger
bidirectional adj	bidirektional
billing	Gebührenverrechnung
binary phase shift keying, BPSK	Zweiphasenumtastung, 2-PSK
bit burst	Bitbündel
~ error probability	Bitfehlerwahrscheinlichkeit
~ error rate	Bitfehlerrate, Bitfehlerhäufigkeit
~ rate	Bitrate, Datenrate
~ suppression	Bitausblendung
~ synchronization	Bitsynchronisation
~-transparent adj	bit-transparent
black-out	Netzzusammenbruch
blank-burst mode	Zeitschlitzeinblendung
blanking interval	Austastlücke
~ signal	Austastsignal
blind occupation	Blindbelegung
block	Block
~ code	Block-Code
~ error probability	Blockfehlerwahrscheinlichkeit
~ error rate	Blockfehlerhäufigkeit, Blockfehlerrate
~-oriented access procedure	blockorientierte Zugangsprozedur
blocked call	blockierter Anruf
blocking	Blockierung
~ function	Sperrfunktion
~ probability	Blockierungswahrscheinlichkeit
~ signal	Sperrsignal
internal ~	innere Blockierung
book vb (a call)	anmelden
both-way transmisstion	beidseitige Übertragung
bothways adj	wechselseitig
~ trunk circuit	wechselseitiger Leitungssatz
branch	Abzweigstelle
~ exchange	Nebenstellenanlage, Zweigamt
private automatic ~ exchange, PABX	private automatische Nebenstellenanlage

private ~ exchange, PBX	private Nebenstellenanlage
~ off point	Abzweigstelle
bridge	Bridge (Verbindung zwischen gleichartigen lokalen Netzen)
broadband (s.a. wideband)	Breitband
~ bus	Breitband-Bus
~ channel	Breitbandkanal
~ communication(s)	Breitbandkommunikation
~ ISDN	Breitband-ISDN (B-ISDN)
~ service	Breitbanddienst
~ switching	Breitband-Vermittlungstechnik
~ switching network	Breitbandkoppelfeld
~ transit exchange	Breitband-Transitvermittlung
~ user line	Breitband-Teilnehmeranschluß
~ videotex	Breitband-Bildschirmtext
broadside array	Querstrahler
broker's call	Makeln
buffer vb	zwischenspeichern
bug	Fehler (im Programm, in der Software)
built-up areas	bebaute Gebiete
burglar alarm	Einbrecheralarm
burst error	Bündelfehler
~ transmission	Burstübertragung
bus	Bus
~ arbiter	Buszuteiler
~ archtitecture	Busstruktur
~ changeover	Umstecken am Bus
~ structure	Busstruktur
~ topology	Bustopologie
~ -type network	Busnetz
busy	belegt
~ condition	Belegtzustand
~ display terminal	Besetztanzeigeterminal
~ hour	Hauptverkehrsstunde, HVStd
~ hour call attempts, BHCA	angebotene Belegungen in der Hauptverkehrsstunde, Belegungsversuche während der Hauptverkehrsstunde
~ hours	Spitzenbelastungszeit

~ indication	Besetztanzeige
~ signal	Besetztzeichen
audible ~ signal	akustisches Besetztzeichen
~ state	Besetztzustand, Belegtzustand
~ tone	Besetztton
~ time	Belegungszeit
busy out vb a subscriber	Sperren eines Teilnehmers
buzzer	Summer
byte	Byte

C

call vb	rufen, anrufen, abrufen
call	Ruf, Anruf, Abruf, Verbindung, Belegung, Gespräch
~ acceptance	Anrufannahme
~ -accepted signal	Rufannahme
~ attempt	Anrufversuch, Verbindungsversuch, Belegungsversuch
busy hour ~ attempts, BHCA	Belegungsversuche während der Hauptverkehrsstunde, angebotene Belegungen in der Hauptverkehrsstunde
~ barring	Sperren von Anrufen
~ booking	Gesprächsanmeldung
~ charge	Gebühr, Fernsprechgebühr, Gesprächsgebühr
~ collision	Belegungszusammenstoß, Rufzusammenstoß, Verbindungszusammenstoß
~ completion rate	Anteil zustandegekommener Verbindungen

~ connected signal	Freizeichen, Verbunden-Signal
~ data	Rufdaten
~ detection	Ruferkennung
~ density	Anrufhäufigkeit
~ diversion	Anrufumleitung, Rufumleitung
~ duration	Gesprächszeit, Verbindungsdauer
average ~ duration	mittlere Verbindungsdauer
chargeable ~ duration	gebührenpflichtige Verbindungsdauer
~ establishment	Verbindungsaufbau
~ fee	Gesprächsentgelt
~ forwarding	Anrufweiterleitung, Rufweiterleitung
unconditional ~ forwarding	bedingungslose Anrufweiterleitung
~ forwarding on mobile subscriber busy, CFMSB	Anrufumleitung im Besetztfall, Anrufweiterleitung bei belegtem Funkanschluß
~ forwarding on mobile subscriber not reachable	Anrufumleitung bei Nichterreichbarkeit
~ forwarding on radio congestion, CFRC	Anrufweiterleitung bei Funküberlastung
~ forwarding on mobile subscriber not registered, CFMSNR	Anrufweiterleitung bei nicht gemeldetem Funkteilnehmer
~ forwarding on no reply, CFNR	Anrufweiterleitung wenn keine Anwort, automatische Anrufweiterschaltung
~ forwarding on no paging response, CFNPR	Anrufweiterleitung wenn keine Antwort auf Melderuf
~ forwarding unconditional	unbedingte Anrufumleitung
~ handling	Gesprächsabwicklung, Rufabwicklung, Verbindungsbearbeitung
~ handling capacity	Leistungsfähigkeit
~ handoff	Anrufweiterschaltung
~ hold	Anrufwarteschleife, Halten einer Verbindung
~ holding operation	Warteschlangenbetrieb, Warteverkehr
~ identification	Rufkennung
~ in progress	bestehendes Gespräch, laufendes Gespräch
~ intent	Verbindungswunsch, Anrufabsicht, Bedienungswunsch
~ load sharing	Belastungsteilung, Teilung der Verkehrslast, Lastverteilung

~ load sharing mode	Lastteilverfahren
~ maintenance	Verbindungsaufrechterhaltung
~ meter	Gesprächszähler
~ metering	Gebührenerfassung
~-not-accepted signal	Rufabweisung
~ number	Rufnummer
personal ~ number	persönliche Rufnummer
personalized ~ number	personenorientierte Rufnummer, personenbezogene Rufnummer
~ number display	Rufnummernanzeige
~ number memory	Rufnummernspeicher
~ park	Parkschaltung
~ parking	Parken (einer Verbindung)
~ pattern	Belegungsmuster
~ pickup	Anrufübernahme
~ processing	Anrufverarbeitung, Verbindungsbearbeitung
~-processing integration	vermittlungstechnische Integration
~-processing message	vermittlungstechnische Meldung
~-processing periphery	vermittlungstechnische Peripherie
~-processing rate	Vermittlungsleistung
~-processing sequence	vermittlungstechnischer Ablauf
~-processing software	vermittlungstechnische Software
~-progress tone, CPT	Hörton
~ pulse	Abrufimpuls
~ quality	Verbindungsqualität, Gesprächsqualität
~ queuing	Warteschlangenbetrieb
~ quota allocation table	Quotierungstabelle
~ rate overflow	Rufanzahlüberschreitung
~ re-establishment	Wiederaufnahme der Verbindung
~ request	Rufanforderung, Verbindungsanforderung, Verbindungswunsch
~ restriction	Gesprächsbegrenzung
~ routing	Rufleitweglenkung
~ setup	Verbindungsaufbau
off-air ~ setup, OACSU	Verbindungsaufbau ohne Sprechkanalbelegung, sprechkanalfreier Verbindungsaufbau
~ setup procedure	Rufaufbauprozedur
~ setup time	Rufaufbauzeit
~ supervision	Verbindungsüberwachung

~ throughput rate   Durchschalteleistung
   malicious ~ identification   Fangen
   malicious ~ identification data   Fangdaten
~ tracing   Fangen
~ tracing data   Fangdaten
~ transfer   Anrufweiterschaltung, Gesprächsweiterverbindung
   automatic ~ unit   automatische Wähleinrichtung (im Datenverkehr)
~ waiting   Anklopfen
~ waiting with call number indication   Anklopfen mit Anzeige
   automatic ~ distributor   automatischer Anrufverteiler
   automatic ~ maker   automatisches Anrufgerät
   abandoned ~   abgebrochener Anruf
   acoustic ~ waiting indication   akustisches Anklopfen
   blocked ~   blockierter Anruf
   carried ~   angenommene Belegung
   chargeable ~   gebührenpflichtiger Anruf
   cold ~   unangemeldeter Anruf
   collect ~   R-Gespräch
   completed ~   zustandegekommener Anruf, zustandegekommene Verbindung
   delayed ~   verzögerte Belegung
   dropped ~   abgebrochener Anruf
   effective ~   zustandegekommene Verbindung
   inadmissible ~   nicht zugelassene Verbindung
   incoming ~   ankommender Anruf, eingehender ~
   ineffective ~   erfolgloser Anruf, nicht zustandegekommene Verbindung
   land-to-mobile ~   ankommende Verbindung
   local ~   Ortsgespräch, Ortsverbindung
   lost ~   abgewiesene Belegung, zurückgewiesene Verbindung, nicht zur Verbindung führender Ruf, Verlustbelegung
   misdirected ~   fehlgeleiteter Anruf
   mobile-originated ~   abgehender Anruf
   mobile-terminated ~   ankommender Anruf, eingehender ~
   mobile-to-land ~   abgehende Verbindung
   mobile-to-mobile ~ s   Anrufe zwischen Mobilfunkteilnehmern

new-~ rate	Rufleistung
no-charge ~	gebührenfreier Anruf
non-dialled ~	Ruf ohne Wahl
offered ~	angebotene Belegung
operator-assisted ~	platzvermittelte Verbindung
operator-initiated ~	platzvermittelte Verbindung
optical ~ waiting indication	optisches Anklopfen
outgoing ~	abgehender Anruf
parked ~	geparkte Verbindung
repeated ~	wiederholter Verbindungsversuch
revenue ~	gebührenpflichtiger Anruf
selective ~	selektiver ~
successful ~	erfolgreich abgewickelter Anruf, erfolgreiche Belegung
uncompleted ~	nicht zustandegekommene Verbindung
uncompleted ~ due to busy condition	wegen Besetztseins nicht zustandegekommene Verbindung
unsuccessful ~	erfolgloser Anruf
waiting ~	wartende Belegung
to answer a ~	einen Anruf entgegennehmen, einen Anruf beantworten
to ~ back	zurückrufen, rückfragen
to camp a ~ onto a trunk	in Wartestellung schalten
to establish a ~	Verbindung herstellen
to make a ~	anrufen
to set up a ~	Verbindung herstellen
callback	Rückruf
~ connection	Rückrufverbindung
~ on busy (completion of calls to busy subscribers)	Rückruf im Besetztfall
~ path	Rückrufweg
~ request	Rückrufauftrag
called line identification, CLI	gerufene Anschlußkennung, Identifizierung der gerufenen Leitung
~ party	gerufener Teilnehmer
~ station	Gegenstelle, Gegenfunkstelle
~ subscriber	gerufener Teilnehmer
caller	Anrufer, rufender Teilnehmer
priority ~	bevorrechtigter Anrufer

calling area	Funkrufbereich
~ channel	Rufkanal
~ line identification, CLI	rufende Anschlußkennung, Identifizierung der rufenden Leitung
~ line identification presentation	Anzeige der Nummer des rufenden Teilnehmers
~ line identification restriction	Unterdrückung der Anzeige der Nummer des rufenden Teilnehmers
~ number identification presentation, CNIP	Anzeige der rufenden Nummer
~ number identification restriction, CNIR	Anzeige der rufenden Nummer gesperrt
~ party	Anrufer, rufender Teilnehmer
~ party pays principle	Prinzip „rufender Teilnehmer zahlt"
~ pattern	Gesprächsverhalten
~ rate	Verbindungshäufigkeit
~ signal	Anrufsignal
~ subscriber	rufender Teilnehmer
camp vb on busy	in Wartestellung schalten
~ a call onto a trunk	in Wartestellung schalten
camp-on	Warten, Anklopfen
~ call	Gespräch in Wartestellung
~ function	Anrufwartefunktion
acoustic ~	akustisches Anklopfen
visual ~	optisches Anklopfen
cancellation completed	Löschungsvollzug
~ request	Löschungsanforderung
candidate cells	andere in Frage kommenden Funkzonen
card telephone	Kartentelefon
carphone	Autotelefon
car telephone	Autotelefon
carrier	Träger, Fernmeldebetriebsgesellschaft, Betreiber, Betreibergesellschaft
~ channel	Trägerkanal
~ circuit	Trägerleitung
~ company	Fernmeldebetriebsgesellschaft

~ failure alarm — Alarm bei Trägerausfall
~ frequency — Trägerfrequenz
modulate vb to a ~ frequency — auf eine Trägerfrequenz modulieren
~ frequency offset — Trägerfrequenzversatz
~ line — Trägerleitung
~ repeater — Trägerstromverstärker
~ sense multiple access with collision detection, CSMA/CD — Mehrfachzugriff mit Kollisionserkennung
~-to-interference ratio, C/I ratio, CIR — Träger-Störleistungsverhältnis
~-to-noise ratio, CNR, C/N ratio — Träger-Rausch-Abstand, Träger-Rauschleistungsverhältnis
~ wave — Trägerwelle
audio tone frequency shift modulated ~ — FSK-Träger

catastrophe class of service, ~ privilege — Katastrophenberechtigung

category of access — Zugangsart

CB radio, citizens' band radio — Jedermann-Funk

CCIR (Comité Consultatif International des Radiocommunications) — internationaler beratender Ausschuß für den Funkdienst

CCITT (Comité Consultatif International Télégraphique et Téléphonique) — internationaler beratender Ausschuß für den Telegrafen- und Fernsprechdienst

CCITT standard — CCITT-Empfehlung

cell, radio cell — Funkzone, Funkzelle, Zone, Zelle
~ boundary — Funkzonengrenze
~ by cell — funkzonenweise
~ change — Funkzonenwechsel
~ change request — Umbuchantrag
~ configuration — Funkzonenkonfiguration
~ coverage area — Funkzonenversorgungsbereich
~ identity — Funkzonenkennung
~ overlay — Funkzonenüberlagerung

~ placement | Funkzonenzuordnung
~ radius (Plural: radii) | Funkzonenradius
~ sectorization | Zonensektorierung
~ site | Zellenstation
~ spacing | Funkzonenabstand
~ splitting | Funkzonenunterteilung, Zellteilung
~ subdivision | Funkzonenunterteilung
  candidate ~ s | andere in Frage kommenden Funkzonen
  overlaid ~ | überlagerte Funkzone
  serving ~ | versorgende Zone
  underlaid ~ | unterlagerte Funkzone

cellular coverage | Versorgung mit dem Zellularsystem
~ mobile radio | zellularer Mobilfunk
~ mobile telephone system | zellulares Funkfernsprechsystem
  digital ~ network | digitales Zellularnetz
~ network structure | zellulare Netzstruktur
~ phone service | zellularer Telefondienst
~ radio network | zellulares Funknetz
~ radio system | zellulares Funksystem
~ radio telephone system | zellulares Funkfernsprechsystem
~ radio telephony | Zellulartelefonie
~ services | Zellulardienste
~ subscriber | Teilnehmer am zellularen Mobilfunk
~ system | Zellularsystem, zellulares Funksystem

CEPT (Conférence Européenne des Administrations des Postes et Télécommunications)
European Conference of Postal and Telecommunications Administrations | Europäischer Zusammenschluß der Post- und Fernmeldeverwaltungen

central request lockout | zentrale Anforderungssperre
~ switch | Zentralvermittlungsstelle
certificate of conformity | Konformitätsbescheinigung
chaining of features | Kettung von Leistungsmerkmalen
change of service | Dienstewechsel

channel	Kanal
~ alignment	Kanalabgleichung
~ assignment	Kanalzuteilung
fixed ~ assignment	feste Kanalzuteilung
flexible ~ assignment	flexible Kanalzuteilung
~ -associated signalling	kanalgebundene Zeichengabe, kanal-individuelle Zeichengabe
~ capacity	Kanalkapazität
~ event	Kanalanreiz
~ group	Kanalbündel
~ization	Kanalausstattung, Kanaleinteilung
~ set	Kanalbündel
~ spacing	Kanalabstand, Nachbarkanalabstand
~ status bit	Kanalzustandsbit
~ switching	Kanaldurchschaltung
adjacent ~	benachbarter Kanal, Nachbarkanal
adjacent ~ interference	Störung durch Nachbarkanal
co- ~	Gleichkanal
common ~	zentraler Kanal
common- ~ signalling	Zeichengabe mit gemeinsamem Zeichenkanal
dedicated ~	festgeschalteter Kanal
half-rate ~	Kanal mit halber Bitrate
character	Zeichen
~ error probability	Zeichenfehlerwahrscheinlichkeit
~ repertoire	Zeichensatz, Zeichenvorrat
~ request	Zeichenanforderung
~ set	Zeichensatz, Zeichenvorrat
~ timing	Zeichentakt
charge	Gebühr
~ display	Gebührenanzeige
~ indicator	Gebührenanzeiger, Gebührenzähler
~ meter	Gebührenanzeiger, Gebührenzähler
~ metering	Gebührenerfassung
~ registration	Gebührenzählung, Gebührenerfassung
~ structure	Gebührenstruktur
low- ~ period	gebührengünstige Zeit
advice of ~	Gebührenanzeige
activation ~	Anschlußgebühr, Bereitstellungsgebühr
establishing ~	Bereitstellungsgebühr pro Verbindung

fixed monthly ~	feste monatliche Gebühr
non-recurring activation ~	einmalige Bereitstellungsgebühr
non-recurring ~	einmalige Gebühr
one-time ~	einmalige Gebühr
chargeable call	gebührenpflichtiger Anruf
~ minutes	Gebührenminuten
notification of ~ time	Gebührenzuschreiben
charging by time	Gebührenbemessung (nach Dauer)
~ area	Gebührenzone
reversed ~	Gebührenübernahme
reverse ~	R-Gespräch
check-in vb	anmelden, einbuchen
check-in file	Aktivdatei
~ request	Einbuchungsauftrag
chip card	Chipkarte
~-card reader	Chipkarten-Leser
~-card telephone	Chipkarten-Fernsprecher, Kartentelefon
circuit	Leitung, Satz (Verbindungssatz), Verbindung
~ group	Satzgruppe
~-switched adj	leitungsvermittelt
~-switched network	leitungsvermitteltes Netz
~-switched public data network, CSPDN	leitungsvermitteltes öffentliches Datennetz
~ switching, CS	Durchschaltevermittlung, Leitungsvermittlung
dedicated ~	festgeschaltete Leitung
permanent virtual ~	feste virtuelle Verbindung
switched virtual ~	gewählte virtuelle Verbindung
zero-loss ~	verlustlose Leitung
circular waveguide	Rundhohlleiter
citizens' band radio, CB radio	Jedermann-Funk
class-C amplifier	C-Verstärker
class of service	Benutzerklasse, Berechtigungsklasse Teilnehmerbetriebsklasse
~-of-service code	Klassenkennzeichnung

clear vb (a connection)	abbauen, auflösen (Verbindung)
~ down vb	abbrechen (Verbindung)
~ (a fault)	beseitigen (Fehler, Störung), entstören
clearback signal	Schlußzeichen
clearing house	Verrechnungsstelle
~ signal	Schlußzeichen
clear-down	Abbruch
click vb	knacken
~ noise	Knackstörung
~ rate	Knackrate
clock vb	takten
clock	Takt
~ and synchronizing pulse	Takt- und Synchronisationsimpuls
~ generator	Taktgeber
~ pulse	Taktimpuls
internal network ~	netzinterner Takt
~-independent	nicht taktgebunden
~-pulse controlled	taktgebunden, taktgesteuert
under ~ control	taktgebunden, taktgesteuert
closed LAN (local area network)	geschlossenes LAN (lokales Netz/Netzwerk)
~ user group	geschlossene Benutzergruppe, geschlossene Teilnehmergruppe
cluster	Funkzonengruppe, Zellbündel, Cluster
~ controller	Cluster-Steuerung
~ size (number of cells per cluster)	Clustermaß, Clustergröße, Clusterzahl
C network	C-Netz (450-MHz-Bereich)
coarse-time clock pulse	Grobtakt
coaxial cable, coax cable	Koaxialkabel, Koax-Kabel
co-channel, common channel	Gleichkanal
~ base station	Gleichkanal-Basisstation, Gleichkanal-Funkfeststation
~ cell	Gleichkanal-Funkzone
~ interference	Gleichkanalstörung
~ operation	Gleichkanalbetrieb

~ protection ratio	Gleichkanalschutzabstand
~ reuse distance	Gleichkanal-Wiederholabstand, Frequenzwiederholabstand
~ reuse ratio	Frequenzwiederbenutzungsfaktor
code digit	Kennziffer
~ division multiple access, CDMA	Vielfachzugriff im Codemultiplex, Vielfachzugriff durch Codemodulation
area ~	Ortsnetzkennzahl
class-of-service ~	Klassenkennzeichnung
code-transparent adj (independent of code structure)	codetransparent
coherence bandwidth	Kohärenzbandbreite
coinbox telephone, DDD coinbox telephone	Fernmünzer, Münzfernsprecher
coin validation	Münzerkennung
cold call	unangemeldeter Anruf
collect call	R-Gespräch
collision	Kollision, Zusammenstoß, Konflikt
call ~	Verbindungszusammenstoß
head-on ~	Verbindungszusammenstoß
co-located adj	im selben Raum/Gebäude etc. untergebracht
colour telefax	Farbfernkopieren
comail	Computerpost
combination 26 (plus sign)	Schlußkreuz
common air interface	gemeinsame Luftschnittstelle
~ -channel signalling	Zeichengabe mit gemeinsamem Zeichenkanal, Zentralkanal-Zeichengabe
~ -channel signalling system # 7 (CCITT)	Zentralkanal-Zeichengabe-Verfahren Nr. 7
~ mode	Gleichtakt
~ -mode rejection	Gleichtaktunterdrückung
~ serving trunk	gemeinsame Abnehmerleitung
~ signalling channel	zentraler Zeichengabekanal
~ trunk group	gemeinsames Leitungsbündel

communication protocol   Kommunikationsprotokoll
   internetwork ~   netzüberschreitende Kommunikation
   non-voice ~   nichtsprachliche Kommunikation

communications operating system   Betriebssystem für Datenfernübertragung

~ satellite   Nachrichtensatellit, Fernmeldesatellit (z.B. INTELSAT)

~ security, COMSEC   Sicherheit im Fernmeldeverkehr
~ technology   Nachrichtentechnik

commuting pattern   Pendlerverhalten

compact telephone   Kompakttelefon

compander   Kompander

compatibility   Kompatibilität
~ matrix   Verträglichkeitsmatrix

compensate vb   abgleichen

completed call   zustandegekommener Anruf

completely restricted extension   nicht amtsberechtigte Nebenstelle

component wave   Teilwelle

composite voice and data use   Einsatz im Sprach- und Datenverbund

compress vb   komprimieren

computer-controlled exchange   rechnergesteuerte Vermittlung
~ PABX circuit   Datenverbundleitung

computerized tracking   elektronische Verfolgung

concentration, area of industrial ~   Ballungsgebiet (Gewerbe und Industrie)

concentrator   Konzentrator

conference call   Konferenzverbindung
~ calling   Konferenzgespräch, Telefon-Konferenz

~ circuit   Konferenzschaltung
~ connection   Konferenzverbindung
~ repeater   Konferenzverstärker
~ service   Konferenzschaltung
telephone ~   Telefon-Konferenz

configuration level	Ausbaustufe
conflicting event	gegenteiliger Anreiz
conformity	Konformität
certficate of ~	Konformitätsbescheinigung
congestion	Überbelegung, Überlastung
connect vb radially	sternförmig verbinden
~ ed	Verbindung hergestellt
~ through	verbinden, durchverbinden, durch- schalten
~ -when-free facility	verbinden wenn frei
connected line identification restriction	Unterdrückung der Anzeige der Nummer des gerufenen Teilnehmers
~ line identification presentation	Anzeige der Nummer des gerufenen Teilnehmers
~ number identification presentation, ConNIP	Anzeige der gerufenen Nummer
~ number identification restriction, ConNIR	Anzeige der gerufenen Nummer gesperrt
connecting delay	Verbindungsherstellzeit
connection	Verbindung
~ cleardown	Verbindungsabbau
~ privilege	Berechtigung
~ setup direction	Verbindungsaufbaurichtung
~ setup time	Aufbauzeit (einer Verbindung)
~ status data	Verbindungszustandsdaten
circuit-switched ~	leitungsvermittelte Verbindung
direct station-to-station ~	direkt durchgeschaltete Verbindung
disrupted ~	unterbrochene Verbindung
incomplete ~	unvollendete Verbindung
to clear a ~	Verbindung auflösen
to clear down a ~	Verbindung abbauen
to establish a ~	Verbindung herstellen
to set up a ~	Verbindung herstellen
constant availability	konstante Erreichbarkeit, konstante Verfügbarkeit
consultation	Rückfrage
~ line circuit	Rückfrage-Teilnehmerschaltung
container installation	Container-Vermittlungsstelle

contention | Konflikt
~ control | Kondliktauflösung
~ mode | Konkurrenzbetrieb

continuity | Durchgang
   test vb for continuity | auf Durchgang prüfen

continuous cycle request | Dauerzyklusanforderung
~ phase frequency shift keying, CPFSK | kontinuierliche Phasen-Frequenz-umtastung
~ receive state | Dauerempfangszustand
~ request | Daueranforderung
~ 400 µs timing signal | Dauermäander

control | Steuerung
~ and display panel | Bedien- und Anzeigefeld
~ channel | Steuerkanal
   dedicated ~ channel | festgeschalteter Steuerkanal
~ clock pulse | Steuertakt
~ enable | Steuerungsfreigabe
~ slope | Regelsteilheit
   stored-program ~ | speicherprogrammierte Steuerung

controlled hunting | Gruppenwahl

controller | Steuerung, Steuergerät

conversion services | Konvertierungsdienste

convert vb | umwandeln, wandeln, konvertieren, umcodieren

~ (signals) with no dc component | gleichstromfrei umcodieren

convolutional coding | Faltungscodierung, Konvolutions-codierung

co-ordination processor | Zentralprozessor

cordless PABX | schnurlose Nebenstellenanlage
~ telephone | schnurloses Telefon

core (cable) | Ader
~ diameter | Kerndurchmesser (Lichtwellenleiter)

correct vb (error) | (Fehler) beheben, beseitigen

correction factor | Korrekturfaktor

correlation bandwidth | Korrelationsbandbreite

~ coefficient	Korrelationsfaktor, Korrelationskoeffizient
~ detection	Korrelationsempfang
~ self-noise	Korrelationseigengeräusch
counting pulse	Zähltakt
coverage	Flächendeckung, Bedeckung, räumliche Ausdehnung eines Netzes, Betriebsbereich, Reichweite, Versorgung, Funkversorgung
~ area	Versorgungsbereich, Funkversorgungsbereich, Betriebsbereich
~ gap	Versorgungslücke
~ overlap	sich überlappende Versorgungsgebiete
~ probability	Versorgungswahrscheinlichkeit
~ rate	Versorgungsgrad
area of radio ~	Funkversorgungsbereich
cellular ~	Versorgung mit dem Zellularsystem
degree of ~	Bedeckungsgrad
full ~	flächendeckende Versorgung
nationwide ~	landesweite Versorgung
population ~	Versorgung der Bevölkerung
portable ~	Versorgung mit tragbaren Funktelefonen
radio ~	Reichweite
credit-card call	Kreditkartengespräch
cross-correlation coefficient	Kreuzkorrelationskoeffizient
~ -country . . .	Überland- . . .
~ modulation	Kreuzmodulation
~ -office	amtsintern
~ check	Sprechkreisprüfung
~ transfer time	übergreifende Transferzeit
crosstalk	Nebensprechen, Übersprechen
~ attenuation	Nebensprechdämpfung, Übersprechdämpfung
cradle	Gabel (Telefon)
CSMA/CD (carrier sense multiple access with collision detection)	Vielfach-Zugriffsverfahren mit Kollisionserkennung
cumulative distribution	Summenhäufigkeit, kumulative Verteilung

current status memory	Aktualitätenspeicher
customer	Teilnehmer
~ handling capacity	bedienbare Teilnehmerzahl
~ recorded information	Hinweisgabe (ankommende Sperre mit Zuschreiben eines Textes)
cycle request	Zyklusanforderung
cylindrical diffraction	Zylinderbeugungsdämpfung

D

D1 network, D1 system	D1-Netz
~ operator	D1-Betreibergesellschaft, D1-Betreiber
D2 operator	D2-Betreibergesellschaft, D2-Betreiber
data channel	Datenkanal
centralized ~ channel	gemeinsamer Datenkanal
~ circuit equipment, DCE	Datenübertragungseinrichtung, DÜE
~ circuit terminating equipment	Datenübertragungseinrichtung
~ communications equipment	Datenfernschaltbaugruppe, Datenübertragungseinrichtung
~ communication network	Datenübermittlungsnetz
~ deviation	Frequenzhub (Daten)
~ escape signal	Datenumschaltesignal
~ link	Übermittlungsabschnitt
~ link layer	Leitungsschicht
~ link protocol	Sicherungsprotokoll
~ multiplexer	Datenmultiplexer
~ network	Datennetz
dedicated ~ network	eigenständiges Datennetz, festgeschaltetes Datennetz
public ~ network	öffentliches Datennetz
public ~ transmission service	öffentlicher Datenübermittlungsdienst
public leased-circuit ~ network	öffentliches Direktrufnetz

~ network identification code, DNIC   Datennetzkennzahl

~ protection   Datenschutz
~ rate   Übermittlungsgeschwindigkeit
~ record   Datensatz
~ security   Datensicherheit
~ selector   Datenweiche
~ services   Datendienste
~ sink   Datensenke (Empfangsstelle)
~ source   Datenquelle (Sendestelle)
~ terminal equipment, DTE   Datenendeinrichtungen, DEE
~ terminal subscriber   Datenteilnehmer
~ transfer rate   Transfergeschwindigkeit
~ transmission services   Datenübermittlungsdienste

Datel service (data telecommunications)   Dateldienst (der Bundespost)

datex service (data exchange)   Datex-Dienst (der Bundespost)
~ line switching network   Datex-L-Netz (Datex-Leitungsvermittlungsnetz)

~ network termination unit   Datexnetz-Abschlußgerät
~ packet switching network   Datex-P-Netz (Datex-Paketvermittlungsnetz)

D channel   D-Kanal (Steuerkanal im ISDN)
~ channel protocol   D-Kanal-Protokoll

dc component, to convert (signals) with no ~ component   gleichstromfrei umcodieren

DDD coinbox telephone (DDD = direct distance dialling)   Fernmünzer

deactivation   Abmeldung
~ request   Abmeldungsantrag

decade selection   Dekadenwahl

decibel, dB   Dezibel, dB

decompress vb   dekomprimieren

decoupler   Entkoppler

dedicated adj   festgeschaltet
~ channel   festgeschalteter Kanal
~ circuit   festgeschaltete Leitung

~ circuit data network	Datenfestnetz
~ control channel, DCCH	festgeschalteter Steuerkanal
~ line	festgeschaltete Leitung, Standleitung
switching matrix for ~ lines	Standleitungskoppler
~ network	eigenständiges Netz
de-emphasis	Deemphasis, Nachentzerrung
deep fade	Tiefschwund
deepsea cable	Hochseekabel
defect	Fehler, Mangel
remedy vb a ~	Fehler beheben
degrade vb (speech quality)	mindern, herabsetzen (Sprachqualität)
degree of coverage	Bedeckungsgrad, Versorgungsgrad
delay	Verzögerung, Wartedauer
~ call handling	Speicherverkehr
~ -Doppler spectrum	Verzögerungs-Doppler-Spektrum
~ power spectrum	Verzögerungs-Leistungs-Spektrum
~ time	Verzögerungszeit
mean ~ of all calls	mittlere Wartedauer aller Belegungen
mean ~ of calls delayed	mittlere Wartedauer der wartenden Belegungen
delayed call	verzögerte Belegung
delivery confirmation	Übergabebestätigung
delta modulation, DM	Deltamodulation
demand assignment	Bedarfszuteilung
~ service	Sofortverkehr
~ test	Bedarfsprüfung
~ traffic	Sofortverkehr
demodulation	Demodulation
demodulator	Demodulator
demultiplex vb	Multiplex auflösen
demultiplexer	Demultiplexer
dependability software	Sicherungssoftware
~ system	Sicherheitstechnik
~ system software	sicherheitstechnische Software
depress vb	drücken (Taste)

deregulation	Deregulierung (Fernmeldemonopol)
descending	absteigend (z.B. Verkehr)
~ path	absteigender Weg
desired channel	Nutzkanal
~ signal	Nutzsignal
desktop facsimile equipment	Tischfernkopierer
destination exchange	Zielamt
~ operator	Gegenamt
~ point code	Code der Zielvermittlungsstelle
detailed billing	Einzelberechnung
developed areas	erschlossene Gebiete
device code	Gerätekennung
diagnostic packet	Diagnosepaket
dial vb	wählen, anwählen (mit Wählscheibe)
dial	Wählscheibe, Nummernscheibe
~ connection	Wählverbindung
~ operation	Wählbetrieb
~ pulse	Nummernscheibenimpuls, Wählimpuls
~ tone	Wählton
dialled broadband (wideband) service	Breitband-Wähldienst
~ traffic	Wählverkehr
dialling	Wahl, Wählen
~ information	Wahlinformationen
direct-~ number	Durchwahlnummer
direct distance dialling, DDD	Selbstwählfernverkehr
direct inward ~ , DID	Durchwahl
with direct inward ~ to the extension	mit Durchwahl bis zur Nebenstelle
direct ~ -in, DDI	Durchwahl
direct outward ~	Durchwahl
interrupted ~	abgesetzte Wahl
on-hook ~	Wahl bei aufliegendem Hörer
~ line	Wählverbindung
dial-up telephone network	Fernsprechwählnetz
dialog control	Dialogsteuerung
~ mode	Dialogbetrieb

dialplate	Nummernscheibe
~ subscriber	Teilnehmer mit Nummernschalterwahl
differential phase shift keying, DPSK	differentiale Phasensprungmodulation, Phasendifferenzumtastung
~ pulse code modulation, DPCM	Differenz-Puls-Code-Modulation
diffraction	Beugung
~ loss	Beugungsdämpfung, Beugungsschwund
~ model	Beugungsmodell
diffuse reflection	diffuse Reflexion
diffusion model	Diffusionsmodell
digital cellular network	digitales Zellularnetz
~ exchange	Digitalvermittlungsstelle
~ interface for radio control	digitale Schnittstelle für die Anbindung von Basisstationen
~ link	Digitalsignalverbindung
~ network	Digitalnetz
~ node	Digitalknoten
~ short range radio	digitaler Kurzwellenfunk
~ path	Digitalsignalverbindung
~ signal processing	digitale Signalverarbeitung
~ switch	digitale Vermittlungsstelle
~ technology	Digitaltechnik
~ telephone network	digitales Fernsprechnetz
~ -to-analog converter,	D/A-Wandler
~ -analog converter, D-A converter	
~ transmission	digitale Übertragung
digitize vb	digitalisieren, digital darstellen
dipole antenna	Dipolantenne
direct broadcasting sattelite	direktstrahlender Satellit
~ call	Direktruf
~ call facility	Direktrufeinrichtung
~ dialling	Direktwahl
~ dialling-in, DDI	Durchwahl
~ distance dialling, DDD	Fernwahl, Selbstwählfernverkehr
~ inward dialling, DID	Durchwahl
~ outward dialling	Durchwahl
~ route	Direktweg
~ station-to-station connection	direkt durchgeschaltete Verbindung

directional antenna	Richtantenne
direction finding	Peilung
directory assistance	Fernsprechauskunft
~ inquiries	Fernsprechauskunft
~ inquiry services	Auskunftsdienste
~ number	Rufnummer
~ of subscribers	Teilnehmerverzeichnis
discard vb	verwerfen
disconnect vb	abschalten (Verbindung) abbrechen (z.B. Protokoll), trennen (Anruf)
disconnect request	Trennanforderung
disconnection	Abbruch
discrete field distribution	diskrete Feldverteilung (Lichtwellenleiter)
~ sampling pulse	Einzelabtastimpuls
dish antenna	Parabolantenne
dispersive fading	dispersiver Schwund
display handling	Anzeigenbedienung
~ paging	Funkruf mit optischer Anzeige, Funkruf mit Textanzeige
~ panel for service signals	Anzeigefeld für Dienstsignale
disrupted connection	unterbrochene Verbindung
distance covered by a network	räumliche Ausdehnung eines Netzes
~ to be covered by a network	räumliche Ausdehnung eines Netzes
~ measurement	Entfernungsmessung
relative ~ measurement	relative Entfernungsmessung
~ ratio, D/R	Abstand zwischen Funkzonen (gleicher Frequenz)
~ zone	Entfernungszone
distant operator	Gegenamt
distortion	Verzerrung
diverse routing	Umleitung
diversity	Diversity
~ gain	Diversity-Gewinn

~ reception	Diversity-Empfang, Mehrfachempfang
~ receiver	Diversity-Empfänger
divert vb	umleiten
D network	D-Netz (900-MHz-Bereich)
domestic traffic	Inlandsverkehr
do-not-disturb service feature	Ruhe vor dem Telefon
Doppler frequency	Doppler-Frequenz
~ power spectrum	Doppler-Leistungsspektrum
~ spread	Doppler-Verbreiterung
double-current keying	Doppelstromtastung
~ refraction	Doppelbrechung (Lichtwellenleiter)
~ seizure	Doppelbelegung
downlink (BS transmits, MS receives)	Abwärtsstrecke (Verbindung von BS zu MS; Strecke vom Satelliten zur Erdfunkstelle)
~ frequency	Abwärtsfrequenz
download vb	fernladen
downpath	Abwärtsstrecke
DRCS (dyamically redefinable character set)	freiprogrammierbarer Zeichensatz
drive vb	ansteuern
drive-in coin telephone	Auto-Münzfernsprecher
dropped call	abgebrochener Anruf
dual-tone multi-frequency signalling	Mehrfrequenzwahlverfahren
duplex	Duplex, Gegensprechen
~ channel	Duplexkanal
~ circuit	Duplexverbindung, duplexfähige Verbindung
~ spacing	Duplexabstand
~ transmission	Duplexübertragung
dynamically redefinable character set	freiprogrammierbarer Zeichensatz
dynamic channel assignment	dynamische Kanalzuteilung
~ range	Dynamikbereich

E

earphone	Hörkapsel
earth station	Bodenstation, Erdfunkstelle
EBCDIC code (8-bit code) (extended binary-coded decimal interchange code)	EBCDIC-Code, erweiterter Binärcode für Dezimalziffern
echo	Echo
objectionable ~	unerwünschtes störendes Echo
~ canceller	Echokompensator
~ channel	Echokanal
~ check	Echoprüfung
~ compensation	Echounterdrückung
~ compensation method	Echokompensationsverfahren
~ plexing	Echobetrieb
~ plex transmission	Echobetrieb
effective antenna height	wirksame Antennenhöhe
~ call	zustandegekommene Verbindung
~ radiated power	äquivalente Strahlungsleistung
electromagnetic compatibility	elektromagnetische Verträglichkeit
~ interference, EMI	elektromagnetische Interferenz
electronic in-house mail	elektronische Hauspost
~ mail	elektronische Post
~ mailbox	elektronischer Briefkasten
	elektronisches Postfach
~ telephone directory	elektronisches Telefonbuch
eliminate vb	beseitigen (Fehler)
emergency call service	Notrufdienst
~ call station	Notrufstelle
~ organization	Notrufträger
~ telephone	Notruftelefon

143

emulate vb	emulieren
emulation service	Emulationsservice
enable vb	freigeben, freischalten
enable decoding	Decodierungsfreigabe
~ signal	Freigabesignal
encrypted access	verschlüsselter Zugang
end-of-selection (+)	Schlußkreuz
~ user	Endbenutzer
E network	E-Netz (1,8-GHz-Bereich)
enhanced-feature service terminal	Komfortbetriebsterminal
~ features	erweiterte Leistungsmerkmale
~ service features	Zusatzdienstmerkmale
~ services	erweiterte Dienste, Zusatzdienste, Mehrwertdienste
~ voice quality	erhöhte Sprachqualität
enhancer	Verstärker
entrance telephone	Türfreisprechstelle
~ telephone system	Türfreisprecheinrichtung
envelope	Enveloppe, Envelope (Bitgruppe zu übertragender Daten, ergänzt durch 1 Zustands- und 1 Synchronisierbit)
~ mode transmission	envelopeweise Übertragung
equal gain diversity	Summendiversity
equality of access	Gleichberechtigung
equalization	Entzerrung
adaptive ~	adaptive Entzerrung
equalizer	Entzerrer
equipment identity register, EIR international mobile station ~ identity, IMEI	Gerätedatei internationale Gerätekennung
erase message	Löschen von Nachrichten

Erlang, Erl (traffic unit)	Erlang, Erl (Einheit des Verkehrswertes einer Leitung) [0 Erl = dauernd frei] [1 Erl = dauernd belegt]
~'s loss formula	Erlangsche Verlustformel
Ermes, European radio messaging system	europaweiter Funkrufdienst
error	Fehler
~ correcting code	fehlerkorrigierender Code
~ detecting code	Fehlererkennungscode
~ detection	Fehlererkennung
~ probability	Fehlerwahrscheinlichkeit
~ protection	Fehlerschutz, Fehlersicherung
~ rate	Fehlerhäufigkeit
~ symptom	Indiz
recurring ~	wieder auftretender Fehler
repetitive ~	wiederholt auftretender Fehler
transient ~	vorübergehender Fehler
escape vb	entweichen (Signale)
establish vb (a connection)	(Verbindung) aufbauen
establishing charge	Bereitstellungsgebühr pro Verbindung
Ethernet (LAN = local area network of Digital, Intel and Xerox)	Ethernet
Eurocard (European standard size printed circuit board)	Europakarte
European coin telephone	Europa-Münzer
~ Communications Satellite System, ECS	europäisches Fernmeldesatellitensystem
~ radio messaging system, Ermes	europaweiter Funkrufdienst
~ radio paging system	europäischer Funkrufdienst, Euro-Signal
~ Telecommunications Standards Institute, ETSI	Institut für europäische Telekommunikationsstandards
pan-~	europaweit
pan-~ GSM standards	europaweite GSM-Standards
event	Anreiz, Ereignis
~-driven	ereignisgesteuert

~ processing Anreizverarbeitung
  conflicting ~ gegenteiliger Anreiz
  incoming ~ ankommender Anreiz
  internal ~ interner Anreiz
  peripheral ~ Anreiz aus der Peripherie
  suspended ~ wartender Anreiz
  verified ~ gesicherter Anreiz

excess path loss Zusatzdämpfung

exchange vb austauschen (Daten)
~ vb status information Betriebsbereitschaft überprüfen

exchange Amt, Vermittlung, Vermittlungsstelle, Zentrale, Austausch
~ area Anschlußbereich der Vermittlungsstelle
~ center Vermittlungsstelle, Zentrale
~ dial tone Amtswählton
~ line Amtsleitung
~ of identifications Kennungsaustausch, Kennungstausch
~ of identification codes Kennungsaustausch, Kennungstausch
  analog ~ analoge Vermittlungsstelle
  answerback ~ Kennungsaustausch, Kennungstausch
  computer-controlled ~ rechnergesteuerte Vermittlungsstelle
  digital ~ digitale Vermittlungsstelle
  higher-ranking ~ übergeordnetes Amt
  local ~ Endamt

execute vb (Befehle) ausführen, (Programm) abarbeiten

expandable adj erweiterungsfähig, ausbaufähig

expansion area Ausbaugebiet

extended binary-coded decimal interchange code, EBCDIC code EBCDIC-Code (8-Bit-Code), erweiterter Binärcode für Dezimalziffern
~ instruction repertoire erweiterter Befehlsvorrat
~ instruction set erweiterter Befehlsvorrat

extension Nebenstelle
~ line Nebenanschluß
  completely restricted ~ nicht amtsberechtigte Nebenstelle
  indirect-access ~ halbamtsberechtigte Nebenstelle
  limited-access ~ halbamtsberechtigte Nebenstelle
  no-access ~ nicht amtsberechtigte Nebenstelle

partially restricted ~	halbamtsberechtigte Nebenstelle
unrestricted ~	voll amtsberechtigte Nebenstelle
~ set	Nebenstellenapparat
with direct inward dialling (DID) to the ~	mit Durchwahl bis zur Nebenstelle
external communications	Auslandsfernmeldedienst
extraction of upstream information	Entnahme von Rückinformationen
extreme traffic load	Extrembelegung

F

facility	(ISDN) Dienstmerkmal
facsimile vb	fernkopieren
facsimile	Fernkopieren
transmit vb (facsimile)	Fernkopie, Faksimile übertragen
~ transmission service	Telefaxdienst
~ unit	Fernkopierer
fade (away) vb	schwinden
fading, fade	Schwund, Fading
~ duration	Schwunddauer
~ -free adj	fadingfrei
~ frequency	Schwundfrequenz
~ rate	Schwundrate
anti-~ device	Schwundminderer
deep ~	Tiefschwund
dispersive ~	dispersiver Schwund
flat ~	Flachschwund
frequency-selective ~	frequenzselektiver Schwund
Rayleigh ~	Rayleigh-Schwund
selective ~	Selektivschwund

short-term ~	Kurzzeitschwund
fade-out	Totalschwund
failsafe	ausfallsicher
non- ~	nicht ausfallsicher
failure	Ausfall, Störung
~ penetration range	Störwirkbreite
~ rate	Ausfallrate
fall-back circuit	Ersatzleitung
far-end crosstalk	Fernnebensprechen
fault	Fehler, Störung
~ clearance	Entstörung
~ detection	Fehlererkennung
~ -tolerant	störungsunempfindlich
clear vb (fault)	(Störung, Fehler) beseitigen
correct vb (fault)	(Fehler) beheben
eliminate vb (fault)	(Fehler) beseitigen
features	Leistungsmerkmale
chaining of ~	Kettung von Leistungsmerkmalen
enhanced ~	erweiterte Leistungsmerkmale
fee	Gebühr
feedback	Rückmeldung
fiber, fibre	Ader, Faser (Lichtwellenleiter)
~ attenuation	Faserdämpfung
~ buffer	Faserhülle
~ cladding	Fasermantel
~ loss	Faserdämpfung
~ optic cable	Glasfaserkabel, Lichtwellenleiterkabel
~ optics	Lichtleittechnik, Lichtwellenleitertechnik, Faseroptik
all-glass ~	Ganzglasfaser
optical ~ cable	Lichtwellenleiterkabel
field calibration	Feldeichung
discrete ~ distribution	diskrete Feldverteilung
~ service	Außendienst
~ strength	Feldstärke
file server	Dateiserver
figure-of-eight network	Achternetz, Doppelkreisnetz

final route	Letztweg
fine-time clock pulse	Feintakt
first-choice route	Direktweg, Erstweg
~ -choice trunk group	Direktbündel
~ -come, first-served principle	Abfragegerechtigkeit
five-level code	Fünfercode (Fernschreiben)
~ -level telegraph code	Fernschreib-Code, 5-Bit-Fernschreib-Code
fixed adj	ortsfest, fest
~ channel assignment	feste Kanalzuteilung
~ charge	Grundgebühr
~ -image communication	Festbildkommunikation
~ -image teleconference	Festbild-Telefonkonferenz
~ monthly charge	feste monatliche Gebühr
~ routing	feste Verkehrslenkung
~ transmitter	ortsfester Sender
flat rate	Pauschaltarif
flexible channel assignment	flexible Kanalzuteilung
follow me	Anrufüberführung
~ -me transfer	Besuchsschaltung
forced handoff	Zwangsumschaltung
forward vb	weiterleiten
forwarding	Weiterleitung
four-band inversion	Vierbandvertauschung
~ -wire line	Vierdrahtleitung
frame	Rahmen
adaptive ~ alignment	akaptive Rahmensynchronisierung
~ checking sequence, FCS	Blockprüfzeichenfolge
~ clock	Rahmentakt
~ duration	Rahmendauer
~ length	Rahmenlänge
~ pulsing	Rahmentakt
~ synchronization	Rahmensynchronisation
free	gebührenfrei
~ -channels table	Freigabeliste für Kanäle

~ phone service	gebührenfreie Nummer, Gebührenübernahme (durch gerufenen Teilnehmer)
~ space attenuation	Freiraumdämpfung
~ space path loss	Freiraumdämpfung
~ space propagation	Freiraumausbreitung
~ space transmission loss	Freiraumdämpfung
freeze-image communication	Festbildkommunikation
frequency allocation	Frequenzzuweisung (an Dienste)
~ allotment	Frequenzverteilung (an Länder, Gebiete)
~ assignment	Frequenzzuteilung (an Funkstellen, Teilnehmer)
~ band	Freqenzband
~ code modulation	Frequenzcodemodulation
~ correlation function	Frequenzkorrelationsfunktion
~ diversity	Frequenzdiversity
~ -division . . .	frequenzgeteilt
~ division multiplex access, FDMA	FDMA-Zugriffsverfahren, Vielfachzugriff im Frequenzmultiplex
~ -division multiplex grouping	Frequenzmultiplexbündelung
~ -division multiplex connection	Frequenmultiplexverbindung
~ -division multiplexing, FDM	Frequenzmultiplexverfahren
~ economy	Frequenzökonomie
~ frogging	Bändertausch, Bandumsetzung
~ hopping	Frequenzsprungverfahren
~ modulation	Frequenzmodulation
random ~ modulation	stochastische Frequenzmodulation, ausbreitungsbedingte Frequenzmodulation
~ multiplexer	Frequenzmultiplexer
~ range	Frequenzbereich
~ reuse	Frequenzwiederholung, Frequenzwiederbenutzung
~ -selective adj	frequenzgefiltert, frequenzselektiv
~ -selective fading	frequenzselektiver Schwund
~ -sensitive adj	frequenzabhängig
~ separating filter	Frequenzweiche
~ shift	Frequenzhub
~ shift keying, FSK	Frequenzumtastung

~ spectrum	Frequenzspektrum
~ stability	Frequenzstabilität
~ -stabilized adj	frequenzkonstant
~ swing	Frequenzhub
allocate vb frequencies	Frequenzen zuweisen
allot vb ~	Frequenzen verteilen
assign vb ~	Frequenzen zuteilen

Fresnel zone — Fresnelzone

front-end noise — Eingangsrauschen
~ -end processor — Vorrechner, Datenübertragungsvorrechner
~ -to-back ratio — Rückstrahldämpfung
~ -to-end ratio — Rückstrahldämpfung

full availability — volle Erreichbarkeit, volle Verfügbarkeit

~ coverage — flächendeckende Versorgung
~ -coverage network — flächendeckendes Netz
~ duplex — Duplex
~ -duplex transmission — Duplexübertragung
~ -motion video communications — Bewegtbildkommunikation
~ video teleconference — Bewegtbild-Telefonkonferenz
~ -wave dipole — Ganzwellendipol

function sharing — Funktionsteilung

functional orgnanization — funktionelle Gliederung

fuzzy logic — Fuzzy-Logik, "unscharfe" Logik

G

gain (antenna)	Gewinn, Leistungsgewinn
~ control	Verstärkungsregelung
garbled adj	verstümmelt
gateway	Gateway (Verbindung von ungleichen Netzen), Netzkoppler, Durchgangsleitung
~ exchange	Kopfamt
~ mobile services switching center, ~ MSC	Einstiegs-Mobilvermittlungsstelle, Eingangs-Mobilvermittlungsstelle
~ MSC	Einstiegs-MSC, Eingangs-MSC
~ mobile switching center	Koppler-Mobilvermittlungsstelle
international ~ center	internationales Kopfamt
international ~ exchange	internationales Kopfamt
Gaussian minimum shift keying	GMSK-Modulationsverfahren
general interface	Mehrzweckschnittstelle
~ -purpose interface bus, GPIB	IEC-Bus
~ switched telephone network	öffentliches Fernsprechwählnetz
gentex (general telegraph exchange)	Gentex-Dienst (USA)
geostationary orbit	geostationäre Umlaufbahn
~ satellite	geostationärer Satellit
glass fiber	Glasfaser
global area network	Weltkommunikationsnetz
go off-hook vb	abheben, abnehmen (Hörer)
~ on-hook vb	auflegen
grade of service	Betriebsgüte, Dienstgüte, Verkehrsgüte
~ of switching performance	Vermittlungsgüte

gradient index fiber	Gradientenprofilfaser
~ -index optical waveguide	Gradientenwellenleiter
grazing incidence	streifender Einfall
ground-based adj	erdgebunden
ground radio station	Bodenfunkstelle
~ wave	Grundwelle
group alarm frame	Gruppensignalrahmen
~ delay time	Gruppenlaufzeit
~ delay distortion	Gruppenlaufzeitverzerrung
~ index	Gruppenbrechzahl (Lichtwellenleiter)
~ paging	Gruppenruf
~ selection	Gruppenauswahl, Gruppenwahl
~ selector	Gruppenwähler
GSM (Group Spéciale Mobile)	GSM (CEPT-Unterausschuß für europäische Mobilfunkdienste)
~ conformity	GSM-Konformität
~ standards	GSM-Standards, GSM-Normen
pan-European ~ standards	europaweite GSM-Standards

half-duplex	Halbduplex
~ -rate channel	Kanal mit halber Bitrate
Hamming distance	Hamming-Abstand
hand-carried transceiver	Handsprechfunkgerät
handheld phone	Handtelefon
~ mobile station	Hand-Mobilstation
~ portable telephone	Handtelefon
handle vb traffic	Verkehr abwickeln

handoff	Anrufweiterschaltung, Weiterreichvorgang, Verbindungsübergabe, Gesprächsumschaltung
automatic ~	Gesprächsweiterleitung (bei Funkzonenwechsel)
intercell ~	Externumschaltung
inter ~	Externumschaltung
intracell ~	Internumschaltung
intra ~	Internumschaltung
handover	Weiterreichen
~ criterion	Weiterreichkriterium
~ event	Weiterreichvorgang
~ execution	Durchführung des Weiterreichvorgangs
~ request	Weiterreichanforderung
~ strategy	Weiterreichstrategie
intercell ~	Weiterreichen der Verbindung, Externumschaltung, Interzonen-Weiterreichen
intracell ~	Internumschaltung, Intrazonen-Weiterreichen
missed ~	nicht zustandegekommener Weiterreichvorgang
hand portable	Handtelefon, Hand-Mobilstation
handset	Hörer
hands-free operation	Freisprechen
~ -free talking	Freisprechen
~ -free telephone	Freisprechapparat
handshake vb	Quittung austauschen
handshaking	Quittungsaustausch, Quittungsbetrieb, einleitender Datenaustausch
~ signal	Abstimmungszeichen
harmonic distortion	Klirren
~ distortion factor	Klirrfaktor
head end	Kopfstelle
~ -on collision	Belegungszusammenstoß, Verbindungszusammenstoß
heterodyne reception	Heterodyn-Empfang, Überlagerungsempfang

high-calling-rate subscriber Vielsprecher
~ density bipolar code HDBn-Code
~ -gain antenna Antenne mit hohem Gewinn
~ -level data link control, HDLC codeunabhängiges Steuerungsverfahren
~ -pass filter Hochpaß
~ -power base station Großleistungs-Basisstation
higher-level protocol höheres Protokoll
~ -level services höhere Dienste
~ -ranking exchange übergeordnetes Amt
hold vb the line am Apparat bleiben
hold for inquiry Rückfrage
holding time Belegungsdauer, Belegungszeit
  mean ~ time mittlere Belegungsdauer
home exchange Heimat-Funkvermittlungsstelle
~ location register, HLR Heimatdatei
~ mobile services switching center, ~ MSC Heimat-Funkvermittlungsstelle, Heimat-MSC
~ mobile services switching center area, ~ MSC area Heimatbereich
~ position Ausgangsstellung, Grundstellung
~ public land mobile network, ~ PLMN Heimat-Netz
~ region Heimatbereich
homing method Homing-Verfahren
  search with ~ Suchverfahren mit Nullstellung
homogeneous network homogenes Netz
hop length Funkfeldlänge
horn radiator Trichterstrahler
~ -reflector antenna Hornparabolantenne
host, host computer Verarbeitungsrechner
hot-line service Hot-line-Service, selbsttätiger Verbindungsaufbau
hot standby Bereitschaftsbetrieb
~ standby method Hot-standby-Verfahren
hum vb brummen

hum suppression	Brummunterdrückung
hunt vb	suchen, absuchen
hunt group	Sammelanschluß
hunting	Freiwahl
~ position	Suchstellung
~ sequence	Absuchreihenfolge
line ~ method	Suchverfahren für Leitungsbelegung
hybrid, hybrid circuit	Gabelschaltung

I

identification	Identifizierung, Kennung
called line ~	Identifizierung der gerufenen Leitungen
calling line ~	Identifizierung der rufenden Leitungen
exchange of ~ codes	Kennungsaustausch, Kennungstausch
exchange of ~ s	Kennungsaustausch, Kennungstausch
malicious call ~	Identifizierung bösartiger Anrufe
personal ~ number, PIN	persönliche Kennummer
identity	Kennung
IEC (International Electrotechnical Commission)	internationale Normungsorganisation für die Elektrotechnik
IEEE (Institute of Electrical and Electronics Engineers)	US-Verband der Elektroingenieure und Elektrotechniker
ignore vb	verwerfen
illumination (antenna)	Ausleuchtung
image communications	Bildkommunikation
~ frequency	Spiegelfrequenz

impose vb silence	Funkstille auferlegen
impress vb (voltage)	(Spannung) einprägen
inaccessible adj	nicht benutzbar, nicht zugänglich
inadmissible call	nicht zugelassene Verbindung
in-band signalling	Imband-Signalisierung
inbound	ankommend, eingehend
~ traffic	ankommender Verkehr, kommender Verkehr
incoming	ankommend, eingehend
~ call	ankommender Anruf, eingehender Anruf, ankommende Verbindung
~ call log	Anrufliste
~ event	ankommender Anreiz
~ seizure	kommende Belegung
~ traffic	ankommender Verkehr, kommender Verkehr
incomplete connection	unvollendete Verbindung
index of refraction	Brechungskoeffizient
indirect-access extension	halbamtsberechtigte Nebenstelle
individual call verification	Einzelgesprächsnachweis
~ communication	Individualkommunikation
ineffective call	erfolgloser Anruf, nicht zustandegekommene Verbindung
information channel	Datenkanal
~ comparator	Informationsvergleicher
~ content	Informationsgehalt, Nachrichtengehalt
~ frame	Informationsrahmen
~ provider	Informationsanbieter (Btx)
~ service	Informationsdienst, Auskunftsdienst
interexchange ~	Zeichenabgabeverkehr
infrastructure	Infrastruktur
inherent distortion	Eigenverzerrung
inhibit function	Sperrfunktion
~ signal	Sperrsignal
in-house mail	Hauspost
electronic ~-house mail	elektronische Hauspost

initial capacity | Erstausbau (Amt)
~ ly installed capacity | Erstausbau (Amt)
~ startup | Erstinbetriebnahme

inject vb a tone | Ton anlegen

in operation | in Betrieb

input authorization | Eingabeberechtigung
~ matrix | Eingangskoppler
~ -output code converter | Ein-/Ausgabe-Codewandler
~ -output procedure | Ein-/Ausgabe-Prozedur

inquire vb | abfragen

inquiry | Abfrage
~ mode | Abfragemodus
~ phase | Aufforderungsphase zum Senden
~ services | Auskunftsdienste
   directory ~ services | Auskunftsdienste

insertion loss | Einfügungsdämpfung

in service | in Betrieb
~ -service data | Betriebsdaten

instantaneous field strength | Momentanfeldstärke

instruction repertoire | Befehlsvorrat
~ set | Befehlsvorrat
   extended ~ set | erweiterter Befehlsvorrat

integrated broadband communications network | integriertes Breitbandfernmeldenetz
~ broadband telecommunications network | integriertes breitbandiges Fernmeldenetz, IBFN
~ digital network | integriertes digitales Text- und Datennetz, IDN

   wideband ~ fiber optical long-distance communications network | breitbandiges integriertes Glasfaser-Fernmeldenetz, BIGFERN

   wideband ~ optical fiber local communications network | breitbandiges integriertes Glasfaser-Ortsnetz, BIGFON

~ network | Verbundnetz
~ services digital network, ISDN | diensteintegrierendes digitales Netz
~ text and data network | integriertes Text- und Datennetz, IDN

integration	Integration
administration, maintenance and dependability ~	betriebs- und sicherungstechnische Integration
call-processing ~	vermittlungstechnische Integration
INTELSAT (International Telecommunication Satellite)	Internationaler Fernmeldesatellit
interactive adj	Dialog-...
interaction	
acknowledged ~	Dialog mit Quittung
inter-arrival time (of calls)	mittlerer Belegungsabstand
intercell handoff	Externumschaltung, Weiterreichen der Verbindung
~ handover	Interzonen-Weiterreichen
interchange vb	(gegenseitig) austauschen
interchannel crosstalk	Kanalnebensprechen
intercom	Sprechanlage
~ system	Sprechanlage
two-way ~ system	Gegensprechanlage
interconnect vb	zusammenschalten
interconnection	Zusammenschaltung
intercontinental telephone traffic	interkontinentaler Fernsprechverkehr
interexchange information	Zeichenabgabeverkehr
interface vb	anschließen
interface	Schnittstelle
common air ~	gemeinsame Luftschnittstelle
digital ~ for radio control	digitale Schnittstelle für die Anbindung von Basisstationen
general ~	Mehrzweckschnittstelle
internetwork ~	Netz-Netz-Schnittstelle
mobile-station-to-base-station ~	Mobilstation-Basisstation-Schnittstelle
radio ~	Luftschnittstelle
smart ~	intelligente Schnittstelle
user-network ~	Teilnehmer-Netz- ~
V-series ~	V-Serie-Schnittstelle
X-series ~	X-Serie-Schnittstelle
x/y ~	x/y-Schnittstelle

~ converter									Schnittstellenumsetzer
~ expander									Schnittstellenvervielfacher
~ for packet-switched networks				Schnittstelle für Paketvermittlungsnetze
~ multiplier								Schnittstellenvervielfacher
~ requirements								Schnittstellenbedingungen
~ specifications							Schnittstellenbedingungen
~ standard									Schnittstellennorm

interference								Störung, Interferenz
~ area										Störbereich, Störgebiet
~ field strength							Störfeldstärke
~ pattern									Störmuster
~ radiated									Störabstrahlung
~ received									Störeinstrahlung
~ source									Störquelle
~ signal									Störsignal
~ suppression								Entstörung
   adjacent-channel ~			Störung durch Nachbarkanal
   electromagnetic ~			elektromagnetische Interferenz
   intersymbol ~				Nachbarzeichenstörung

interfering signal							Störsignal

interhandoff								Externumschaltung

interleaved channel							Versatzkanal
~ coding									Spreizungscodierung

intermediate node							Transitknoten

intermodulation, IM							Intermodulation
~ interference								Intermodulationsstörung

internal blocking							innere Blockierung
~ event										interner Anreiz
~ network clock								netzinterner Takt
~ network timing							netzinterner Takt

international DDD							Auslandsfernwahl
~ gateway center							internationales Kopfamt, Auslandsvermittlungsstelle
~ gateway exchange							internationales Kopfamt, Auslandsvermittlungsstelle
~ leased circuit							internationale Mietleitung

~ mobile station equipment identity, IMEI   internationale Gerätekennung
~ mobile subscriber identity, IMSI   internationale Teilnehmerkennung
~ permanent circuit connection   internationale Festverbindung
~ prefix   internationale Zugangskennzahl
~ Radio Consultative Committee (CCIR)   internationaler beratender Ausschuß für den Funkdienst
~ transit exchange   internationale Durchgangsvermittlungsstelle

internetwork communication   netzüberschreitende Kommunikation
~ interface   Netz-Netz-Schnittstelle
inter-nodal line   Zwischenknotenleitung
interpreter circuit   Empfangsauswerter
interrogate vb   abfragen
interrogation test pulse   Abfrageprüfimpuls
interrupted dialling   abgesetzte Wahl
interservice communication   diensteüberschreitende Kommunikation

intersymbol interference, ISI   Nachbarzeichenstörung
interval   Pause, Pausenzeit
interworking equipment, ~ unit   Netzanpassungsgerät
intracell handoff   Internumschaltung
~ handover   Internumschaltung, Intrazonen-Weiterreichen

intra-exchange call   Internverbindung
intrahandoff   Internumschaltung
intra-zone channel reassignment   Internumschaltung
invoke vb   (Prozedur) aufrufen
invoked procedure   aufgerufene Prozedur
invoking procedure   aufrufende Prozedur
irradiation   Einstrahlung
irregular terrain   nicht quasiebenes Gelände

ISDN (integrated services digital network)	ISDN (diensteintegrierendes digitales Netz)
ISDN PABX	ISDN-Nebenstellenanlage
~ user basic access	ISDN-Teilnehmeranschluß
ISO (International Organization for Standardization)	ISO (internationales Normungsgremium)
ISO/OSI reference model	ISO/OSI-Referenzmodell
isotropic antenna	isotrope Antenne
itemized billing	Einzelberechnung

J

jitter	Jitter
~ reducer	Jitterreduzierer

K

keying interval	Tastpause
keyword	Kennwort
knife-edge diffraction	Kantenbeugung

L

LAN (local area network)	LAN (lokales Netz, lokales Netzwerk)
closed ~	geschlossenes LAN
open ~	offenes LAN
landline	ortsfest
landline network	Festnetz
~ subscriber	Festnetzteilnehmer
land mobile radio	beweglicher Landfunk
~ mobile radio service	beweglicher Landfunkdienst
~ mobile station	bewegliche Landfunkstelle
~ radio	Landfunk
~ station	ortsfeste Funkstelle
public ~ mobile network, PLMN	öffentliches mobiles Landfunknetz, öffentliches Mobilfunknetz
~ usage	Flächennutzung
land-to-mobile	ankommend
~ -to-mobile call	ankommende Verbindung
large-area median value	Langstreckenmedianwert
~ cell	Großzone, Großzelle
last-choice route	Letztweg
~ number redialling	Wahlwiederholung
layer	Schicht
~ model	Schichtenmodell
seven- ~ model	Siebenschichtmodell
~ protocol	Schichtenprotokoll
application ~	Anwendungsschicht
link ~	Übertragungsschicht, Datensicherungsschicht

    network ~   Netzwerkschicht, Vermittlungsschicht
    physical ~   physikalische Schicht
    presentation ~   Darstellungsschicht
    session ~   Sitzungsschicht
    transport ~   Transportschicht

lease vb   vermieten, anmieten (Leitungen)

leased circuit   Mietleitung
    international ~ circuit   internationale Mietleitung
~ -circuit data network   Direktrufnetz
~ data circuit terminal   Hauptanschluß für Direktruf
    public ~ -circuit data network   öffentliches Direktrufnetz
~ lines   Mietleitungen, angemietete
                                Übertragungswege

level   Pegel
~ crossing rate, LCR   Schwellenüberschreitungszahl
~ discontinuity   Pegelsprung

lift vb (receiver)   (Hörer) abnehmen, abheben

limited availability   begrenzte Erreichbarkeit, begrenzte
                                Verfügbarkeit
~ -access extension   halbamtsberechtigte Nebenstelle

line   Leitung, Anschluß
    hold vb the ~   am Apparat bleiben
    multiplexed ~   Leitung in Multiplexschaltung

line access procedure   Leitungszugangsverfahren
~ code   Leitungscode
~ concentrator   Leitungskonzentrator
~ connection   drahtgebundene Übertragung
~ enable   Leitungsfreigabe
~ group   Anschlußgruppe, Leitungsbündel
~ hunting method   Leitungssuchverfahren, Suchverfah-
                                ren für Leitungsbelegung
~ interface   Leitungsschnittstelle
~ lockout time   Dauer der unnötigen Belegungen
~ of sight   Sichtlinie
~ -of-sight link   Sichtverbindung
~ -of-sight propagation   Sichtausbreitung
~ scan, ~ scanning   Leitungsabfrage
~ scratchpad entry   Leitungsnotiz

~ seizure	Leitungsbelegung
~ seizure attempt	Belegungsversuch
~ server	Leitungs-Server
~ status signal	Leitungszustandsmeldung
~ switching	Durchschaltebetrieb, Durchschalte-vermittlung
~ utilization degree	Leitungsausnutzungsgrad
leased ~	Mietleitung
line up vb	abgleichen
link vb	anschließen
link	Anschlußleitung, Leitung, Signalverbindung, Zugangspfad, Zwischenleitung, Strecke, Teilstrecke
~ access protocol	Sicherungsprotokoll
~-by-link signalling	abschnittsweise Zeichengabe
~ layer	Datensicherungsschicht, Verbindungsschicht, Übertragungsschicht
data communication ~	Prozessor für Signalisierungssteuerung
data ~ protocol	Sicherungsprotokoll
line-of-sight ~	Sichtverbindung
optical ~	Lichtleitstrecke
listen in vb	mithören
load balancing	Lastausgleich
~ sharing	Lastteilung
loadable software	ladbare Software
local area	Ortsbereich
~ area network, LAN	lokales Netz, lokales Netzwerk, LAN
~ area wideband network	lokales Breitbandnetz
~ area wireless network, Lawn	drahtloses Datennetzwerk
~ call	Ortsgespräch, Ortsverbindung
~ call fee	Ortsgebühr
~ communication network	Ortsverbindungsnetz
~ exchange	Endamt, Endvermittlungsstelle, Ortsamt, Ortsvermittlungsstelle
~ fee zone	Nachbereichszone
~ mean	Kurzstreckenmittelwert, örtlicher Mittelwert

~ network   Ortsnetz
~ node   Ortsknoten
~ office   Ortsvermittlungsstelle
~ operation   Lokalbetrieb
  undisturbed ~ operation   ungestörter Lokalbetrieb
~ procedure error   örtlicher Ablauffehler
~ rate   Ortsgebühr
~ service area   Ortsbereich
~ subscriber   Orts(netz)teilnehmer
~ switch   Ortsvermittlungsstelle
~ switching center   Ortsamt
~ tandem exchange   Ortsdurchgangsvermittlung
~ tariff   Nahtarif
~ time clock   Ortszeituhr
~ traffic   Ortsverkehr
~ zone   Ortszone
location   Standort
~ area, LA   Aufenthaltsbereich
~ area identification, LAI   Standortbereichskennung
~ cancellation procedure, LCP   Standortlöschung
~ identification   Standortkennung
~ information   Standortinformationen
~ information retrieval procedure Aufsuchen der Standortinformationen
~ register, LR   Aufenthaltsdatei, Standortdatei, Teilnehmerdatei
~ registration   Standorterfassung, Ortsregistrierung (Einbuchen in die Standortdatei)
~ registration request   Meldeaufruf
~ tracking   Standortbestimmung, Ortung
~ update   Standortaktualisierung
  self-~   automatische Standorterfassung
locator service   Ortungsdienst
  stolen vehicle ~ service   Ortungsdienst für gestohlene Fahrzeuge

lock out vb   abfangen

log in vb   einbuchen

log off vb   abmelden

log-off   Abmeldung
~-off request   Abmeldeanforderung

log on vb	anmelden, einbuchen
log-on	Anmeldung
~ on request	Anmeldeanforderung
log out vb	ausbuchen
long-distance call	Ferngespräch
~ -distance exchange	Fernamt, Fernvermittlung
~ -distance line	Fernleitung
~ -distance network	Fernnetz
~ -distance switching center	Fernvermittlungsstelle
~ -term median	Langzeitmedianwert
loss-free	verlustlos
loss of radio contact	Abreißen der Funkverbindung
~ probability	Verlustwahrscheinlichkeit
~ relative to free space	Ausbreitungsdämpfung
lost call	abgewiesene Belegung, nicht zur Verbindung führender Ruf, Verlustbelegung
~ call probability	Verlustwahrscheinlichkeit
loud hearing operation	Lauthören
loudspeaker announcement	Lautsprecherdurchsage
low-calling-rate subscriber	Wenigsprecher
~ -charge period	gebührengünstige Zeit
~ er half band	Unterband
~ -noise . . .	störungsarm, geräuscharm
~ -pass filtering	Tiefpaßfilterung
~ -power base station	Kleinleistungs-Basisstation
lower band	Unterband

M

macro language	Makrosprache
switching-oriented ~ language	vermittlungstechnische Makrosprache
magnetic-field switching matrix	Magnetfeldkoppler
mailbox	Briefkasten, Mailbox, Postfach, Telebox
electronic ~	elektronischer Briefkasten
mainframe	Großrechner
main exchange	Hauptvermittlungsstelle
~ station for fixed connection	Hauptanschluß für Direktruf, HfD
~ switch	Knotenvermittlungsstelle
major alarm	dringender Alarm
make vb a call	anrufen
malicious call identification	Fangen, Identifizierung bösartiger Anrufe
~ call identification data	Fangdaten
~ call tracing data	Fangdaten
man-made noise	künstliche Störung
manned exchange	bemanntes Amt
~ operation	bedienter Betrieb
marine radio	Seefunk
maritime mobile service	mobiler Seefunkdienst
mark vb	markieren
mass communication	Massenkommunikation
mast erection	Antennenmastaufbau
~ foundation	Antennenmastfundament

master clock	Haupttakt
match vb	anpassen
matching	Anpassung
maximum integration	Maximumintegration (im ISDN)
mean delay of all calls	mittlere Wartedauer aller Belegungen
~ delay of calls delayed	mittlere Wartedauer der wartenden Belegungen
~ holding time	mittlere Belegungsdauer
~ time between failures, MTBF	mittlerer Ausfallabstand, mittlere Verfügbarkeitsdauer zwischen zwei Ausfällen
~ time between seizures	mittlerer Belegungsabstand
~ traffic carried	mittlere Verkehrsbelastung
~ traffic load	mittlere Verkehrsbelastung
measurement unit	Meßstation
mobile ~ unit	mobile Meßstation
message	Meldung, Nachricht
~ block	Nachrichtenblock
~ cancellation	Löschen von Nachrichten
~ chaining	Nachrichtenverkettung
~ content	Nachrichteninhalt
~ discrimination	Meldungsverteilung
~ handling	Nachrichtenbehandlung
~ prefix signal	Dateneinleitungszeichen
~ routing	Meldungslenkung
~ storage service	Sprachspeicherdienst
~ switching center	Nachrichten-Speichervermittlungsstelle
~ traffic	Nachrichtenverkehr
call-processing ~	vermittlungstechnische Meldung
non-deliverable ~	nicht zustellbare Nachricht
microcell	Kleinstzone, Mikrozelle
~ technology	Mikrozellentechnik
microwave link	Mikrowellenverbindung
~ radio hop	Mikrowellenteilstrecke
mid-air meeting of microwaves	Zusammentreffen von Mikrowellen auf halbem Weg
mid-frequency	Mittenfrequenz

minimum coverage rate	Mindestversorgungsgrad
~ usable field strength	Mindestfeldstärke
misdirected call	fehlgeleiteter Anruf
mispointing (antenna)	Fehlausrichtung
misrouted	fehlgeleitet, falschgeleitet
missed handover	nicht zustandegekommener Weiterreichvorgang
missent	fehlgeleitet, falschgeleitet
mixed code	Mischcode
~ communication	Mischkommunikation
~ -mode communication	Mischkommunikation
~ network	Verbundnetz
~ -structure network	gemischt strukturiertes Netz
mobile adj	beweglich, ortsveränderbar, mobil
mobile access hunting	Suchen eines mobilen Anschlusses, Anrufverteilung
~ communication system	Mobilkommunikationssystem
~ measurement unit	mobile Meßstation
public land ~ network, PLMN	öffentliches Mobilfunknetz
public ~ radio network	öffentliches bewegliches Landfunknetz
public ~ telephone service	öffentlicher beweglicher Landfunkdienst
~ -originated	abgehend, vom Funkteilnehmer abgehend
~ -originated call	abgehender Anruf
~ phone	Funktelefon
~ phone service	Mobilfunkdienst
radio-based ~ phone service	Mobilfunkdienst
~ radio	Mobilfunk, bewegliche Funkdienste
cellular ~ radio	zellularer Mobilfunk
~ radio channel	Mobilfunkkanal
~ radio equipment	Mobilfunkgeräte
~ radio network	Mobilfunknetz
~ radio service	Mobilfunkdienst, beweglicher Funkdienst
~ radio subscriber	Mobilfunkteilnehmer
~ radio system	Mobilfunksystem

~ radio telephone	mobiles Funktelefon
~ radio telephone service	Mobilfunkdienst, Funkfernsprechdienst
~ radio user	Mobilfunkteilnehmer
~ satellite services	mobile Satellitendienste
~ services station	Mobilstation
~ services switching center, MSC	Mobilvermittlungsstelle, Überleiteinrichtung, Funkvermittlungseinrichtung, Funkvermittlungsstelle
~ services switching center area, MSC area	Funkvermittlungsstellenbereich, Funkvermittlungsbereich, MSC-Bereich
~ station, MS	Mobilstation, bewegliche Funkstelle
portable ~ station	tragbare Mobilstation
~ -station-to-base-station interface	Mobilstation-Basisstation-Schnittstelle
transportable ~ station	bewegliche Mobilstation
vehicular ~ station	fahrzeuggebundene Mobilstation
~ station feature	Mobilstations-Leistungsmerkmal
~ subscriber	Mobilfunkteilnehmer, mobiler Teilnehmer
international ~ subscriber identity, IMSI	internationale Teilnehmerkennung
~ subscriber number	Mobilfunkteilnehmernummer, Funktelefonnummer
~ switching center, MSC	Mobilvermittlungsstelle, Funkvermittlungsstelle, Überleiteinrichtung
~ telephone	Funktelefon, Autotelefon
~ telephone service	Funksprechdienst
public ~ telephone service	öffentlicher beweglicher Funkdienst
~ -terminated	ankommend, eingehend, beim Funkteilnehmer ankommend
~ -terminated call	ankommender Anruf, eingehender Anruf
~ -to-base	abgehend
~ -to-land	abgehend
~ -to-land call	abgehende Verbindung
~ -to-mobile call	Anrufe zwischen Mobilfunkteilnehmern
~ transmitter	Übertragungswagen
~ user	Mobilfunkteilnehmer, mobiler Teilnehmer
~ user part	Mobilfunkbenutzerteil

mode, modes pl	Modus, Moden pl (Lichtwellenleiter)
mode of operation	Betriebsart, Betriebsweise
~ change	Betriebsartenwechsel, Betriebswechsel
operating ~	Betriebsart, Betriebsweise
power-up ~	Betriebszustand
modem (modulator/demodulator)	Modem
~ link	Modemstrecke
modular network structure	modulare Netzstruktur
modulate vb to a carrier frequency	auf eine Trägerfrequenz modulieren
modulation method	Modulationsverfahren
module	Modul (Baugruppe)
~ administration and maintenance	Modulbetriebstechnik
~ dependability system	Modulsicherheitstechnik
monitor vb	mithören, überwachen
multi-address call	Sammelruf
~ -address operation	Rundschreibbetrieb
~ -address service	Rundsenden
~ -address call/distribution feature	Rundsenden und Verteilen
multiband antenna	Mehrbereichsantenne
multichannel modem	Mehrkanal-Modem
~ switching	Mehrkanaldurchschaltung
multi-frame mode	Multiblockverfahren
multi-frequency code	Mehrfrequenzcode
~ -frequency signalling	Mehrfrequenzsignalisierung
multi-function modem	Mehrfunktionsmodem
~ -function terminal	Multifunktionsterminal
multi-link procedure	Mehrfachanschlußprozedur
multi-mode fiber	Mehrmodenfaser
multi-party call	Gruppenruf
~ -party facility	Sammelgesprächseinrichtung
multipath channel	Mehrwegekanal
~ fading	Mehrwegeschwund
~ model	Mehrwegemodell

~ propagation	Mehrwegeausbreitung
~ signal	Mehrwegesignal, Umwegsignal
multiple event	Mehrfachanreiz
~ frequency shift keying, MFSK	Mehrfach-Frequenzumtastung
~ scanning	Mehrfachabtastung
~ use of channels	Kanalteilung
multiplex vb	mehrfach ausnutzen
multiplexed line	Leitung in Multiplexschaltung
multiplexer	Multiplexer, Mux
multiplex access	Vielfach-Zugriffsverfahren
~ interface	Multiplex-Schnittstelle
multipoint access	Mehrpunktzugriff
~ connection	Mehrpunktverbindung
~ network	Mehrpunktnetz
multiprocessor mode	Multiprozessorbetrieb
multiservice network	mehrfach genutztes Netz, Netz mit Mehrfachausnutzung
~ operation	Mehrdienstebetrieb
~ terminal	Mehrdienste-Endgerät
multistage network	mehrstufiges Netz
music-on-hold	Beruhigungston, Musikeinspielung im Haltestand
mute vb	abschalten (z.B. Lautsprecher)
mutilated	verstümmelt
muting feature	Stummschaltung

N

name key for speed dialling	Namenstaste für Kurzwahl
narrowband (s. also broadband)	Schmalband
~ communication(s)	Schmalbandkommunikation
~ service	Schmalbanddienst
~ switching network	Schmalbandkoppelnetz
~ transmission	Schmalbandübertragung
national long-distance dialling network, ~ DDD network	Landesfernwahlnetz
~ traffic	Inlandsverkehr
~ trunk exchange	Inlands-Fernvermittlungsstelle
natural noise	naturgegebene Störung, naturgegebene Funkstörung
near-end crosstalk attenuation	Nahnebensprechdämpfung
negative acknowledgement, NAK	negative Quittierung, negative Rückmeldung
network	Netz
circuit-switched ~	leitungsvermitteltes Netz
circuit-switched public data ~, CSPDN	leitungsvermitteltes öffentliches Datennetz
dedicated ~	eigenständiges Netz
full-coverage ~	flächendeckendes Netz
homogeneous ~	homogenes Netz
integrated digital ~	integriertes digitales Netz
local ~	Ortsnetz
local area wireless ~, Lawn	drahtloses Datennetzwerk
local communication ~	Ortsverbindungsnetz
mixed ~	Verbundnetz
mixed-structure ~	gemischt strukturiertes Netz
modular ~ structure	modulare Netzstruktur

multi-service ~ mehrfach genutztes Netz, Netz mit Mehrfachnutzung
narrowband switching ~ Schmalbandkoppelnetz
non-blocking switching ~ blockierungsfreies Koppelnetz
optical fiber ~ Glasfasernetz
packet-switched ~ paketvermitteltes Netz
service-specific ~ dienstspezifisches Netz
switched ~ leitungsvermitteltes Netz
value-added ~ Netz mit erweiterten Übertragungsmöglichkeiten

~ access Netzzugang
~ administration Netzverwaltung
~ architecture Netzarchitektur
internal ~ clock netzinterner Takt
~ clock pulse Netztakt
~ configuration Netzkonfiguration
~ congestion Netzüberlastung
~ construction Netzaufbau
~ -dependent netzabhängig
~ design Netzentwurf
~ diagnosis Netzdiagnose
~ establishment Netzaufbau
~ expansion Netzausbau
~ extension Netzerweiterung
~ failure Netzfehler, Netzstörung, Netzausfall
~ failure report Netzfehlermeldung
~ feature Netzleistungsmerkmal
~ ing Vernetzung
~ interconnection Netzübergänge
~ interfacing Netzanschlußtechnik
~ interface technology Netzanschlußtechnik
~ interworking Netzübergang
~ layer Netzwerkschicht, Vermittlungsschicht
~ level Netzebene
~ management Netzführung, Netzverwaltung
~ management center, NMC Netzverwaltungszentrale
~ management control system Netzverwaltungssteuerung
~ message Netzmeldung
~ node Netzknoten
~ operation Netzbetrieb
~ operator Netzbetreiber

~ processor — Netzwerkprozessor
~ protocol — Netzprotokoll, Netzwerkprotokoll, Vermittlungsprotokoll
~ service — Netzdienst
~ software — Netzsoftware
~ structure — Netzstruktur
   cellular ~ structure — zellulare Netzstruktur
~ termination — Netzabschluß
~ termination unit — Nachrichtenfernschaltgerät, Netzabschlußgerät

   internal ~ timing — netzinterner Takt
~ timing pulse — Netztakt
~ topology — Netztopologie
~ traffic control — Netzverkehrssteuerung
~ user identifier, NUI — Teilnehmerkennung

new-call rate — Rufleistung

NMT (Nordic Mobile Telephone System) — skandinavisches Mobilfunksystem (NMT)

no-access extension — nicht amtsberechtigte Nebenstelle
~-charge call — gebührenfreier Anruf

node — Knoten
~ computer — Knotenrechner
   local ~ — Ortsknoten

noise — Rauschen, Geräusch, Störung
~ factor — Rauschfaktor
~ field strength — Störfeldstärke
~ frequency — Störfrequenz
~-immune — störungsunempfindlich
~ immunity — Rauschunempfindlichkeit
~ level — Störpegel
~ performance — Rauschverhalten
~ spectrum — Störspektrum
~ threshold — Rauschgrenze
   man-made ~ — künstliche Störungen
   natural ~ — naturgegebene Störung, naturgegebene Funkstörung

non-acceptance signal — Abweissignal
~-blocking — blockierungsfrei
~-busy hours — Zeiten niedriger Verkehrsbelastung

~ -chargeable gebührenfrei
~ -chargeable interval Karenzzeit
~ -deliverable message nicht zustellbare Nachricht
~ -dialled call Ruf ohne Wahl
~ -failsafe nicht ausfallsicher
~ -recurring activation charge einmalige Bereitstellungsgebühr
~ -recurring charge einmalige Gebühr
~ -return-to-zero code NRZ-Code, Richtungswechselschrift
~ -switched festgeschaltet
~ -voice communication nichtsprachliche Kommunikation
~ -voice service Nichtsprachdienst, Nicht-Fernsprechdienst

notification Anmeldung
~ of chargeable time Gebührenzuschreibung
~ of transmission errors Fehlerbenachrichtigung
~ for receiver Hinweisgabe (ankommende Sperre mit Zuschreiben eines Textes)

number busy Rufnummer besetzt
~ plate Nummernscheibe
~ plate dialling Nummernwahlschalterwahl
~ redial feature Wahlwiederholung
~ -unobtainable tone, (NU tone) NU-Ton (NU = Nummer unbeschaltet)
  call ~ Rufnummer
  subscriber's ~ Rufnummer

O

objectionable echo	unerwünschtes störendes Echo
occupance	Belegungszustand
~ state	Belegungszustand
occupancy	Belegung
~ time	Belegungszeit
occupied	belegt
ocean cable	Seekabel
off-air	sprechkanalfrei
~-air call setup, OACSU	Verbindungsaufbau ohne Sprechkanalbelegung, sprechkanalfreier Verbindungsaufbau
offer vb	(Vermittlung) anbieten
offered call	angebotene Belegung
~ traffic	Angebot (Verkehr), Verkehrsangebot
offering trunk	Zubringerleitung
~ trunk group	Zubringerbündel
off-hook	abgenommen, ausgehängt
~-hook event	Aushängeanreiz
~ line	nicht angeschlossen, unabhängig
~-peak hours	Zeiten niedriger Verkehrsbelastung
~-peak rate	Billigtarif
~-site paging	öffentliches Funkrufsystem
~ the air	außer Betrieb (Sender)
office communication(s)	Bürokommunikation
omni antenna	Rundstrahlantenne
~ cell	Flächenkleinzone, Zelle mit Rundstrahlantenne

~ operation	Rundstrahlbetrieb
omnidirectional antenna	Rundstrahlantenne
~ system	Flächenkleinzonennetz
one-cell buffer	Einzellenpuffer
~-time charge	einmalige Gebühr
~-way ...	einseitig gerichtet
~-way mode	Einwegbetrieb
on-hook	aufgelegt, eingehängt
~-hook dialling	Wahl bei aufliegendem Hörer
go vb ~-hook	auflegen
~ line	angeschlossen
~-line/standby mode	Aktiv-/Reserve-Betriebsart
~-site paging	privates Funkrufsystem
~ the air	in Betrieb (Sender)
open LAN	offenes LAN
~ listening	Lauthören
~ system interconnection, OSI	Kommunikation offener Systeme
~ systems communications	offene Kommunikation
operate vb	arbeiten, in Betrieb sein, betätigen, (Taste) drücken
ready to ~	betriebsbereit
operating company	Betreibergesellschaft, Betriebsgesellschaft
~ licence	Betriebszulassung
~ mode	Betriebsart, Arbeitsmodus, Betriebsweise
~ surface	Bedieneroberfläche
operation	Betrieb
~al	betriebsbereit
~ and maintenance	Betriebstechnik
~s and maintenance center, OMC	Betriebs- und Wartungszentrum
attended ~	bedienter Betrieb
call holding ~	Warteschlangenbetrieb
in ~	in Betrieb
manned ~	bedienter Betrieb
mode of ~	Betriebsart
privileged ~	privilegierter Betrieb
unattended ~	unbedienter Betrieb

unmanned ~	unbedienter Betrieb
~ s inhibit signal	Betriebssperrsignal
operator	Betreiber, Bediener, Amt, Platz
~ assistance	Platzbeteiligung, Handvermittlung
~ -assisted call	handvermitteltes Gespräch
~ guidance	Bedienerführung
~ -initiated call	handvermitteltes Gespräch
~ inquiry	Bedieneranfrage
telecommunications ~	Fernmeldegesellschaft
private telephone ~	private Fernmeldegesellschaft
public telephone ~	öffentliche Fernmeldegesellschaft
optical call waiting indication	optisches Anklopfen
~ communications technology	optische Nachrichtentechnik
~ fiber	Glasfaser, Lichtwellenleiter
~ fiber cable	Lichtwellenleiterkabel
~ fiber network	Glasfasernetz
~ link	Lichtleitstrecke
~ telecommunications	optische Fernmeldetechnik
~ waveguide	Lichtwellenleiter
~ waveguide cable	Lichtwellenleiterkabel
~ waveguide technology	Lichtwellenleitertechnik
orbit (satellite)	Umlaufbahn
geostationary ~	geostationäre Umlaufbahn
organization	Organisation, Gliederung
functional ~	funktionelle Gliederung
originating exchange	Ursprungsamt, Ursprungsvermittlungsstelle
~ trunk group	Ursprungsbündel
originator	Absender (einer Nachricht)
acknowledgement to ~	Quittierungsgabe zum Absender
OSI (Open Systems Interconnection)	Kommunikation offener Systeme
~ reference model	OSI-Referenzmodell
outage	Ausfall
out-band signalling	Außerbandsignalisierung, Außerband-Zeichengabe
outbound	abgehend, gehend
~ traffic	abgehender Verkehr, gehender Verkehr

outgoing	abgehend, gehend
~ call	abgehender Anruf, abgehender Ruf, abgehende Verbindung
~ /incoming priority	Priorität für abgehende/ankommende Rufe
~ line	Sendeleitung
~ seizure	gehende Belegung
~ time slot	Ausgangszeitlage
~ traffic	abgehender Verkehr, gehender Verkehr
~ trunk	Sendeleitung
outlying areas	abgelegene Gebiete
out-of-band emission	Außerband-Emission
out-of-order condition	Gestörtzustand, Störzustand
~ -of-order tone	Gestörtzeichen, Störzeichen
~ of service	außer Betrieb
output port	Ausgangspunkt
~ power	Sendeleistung
overall system status	Gesamtsystemstatus
over-channelize vb	überkanalisieren
~ dimensioning	Überdimensionierung
~ flow traffic	Restverkehr
~ head data	vermittlungstechnische Daten
~ laid cell	überlagerte Funkzone
~ load	Überlastung
~ reach interference	Überreichweitenstörung
~ time rate	Folgegebühr
overlaid cell	überlagerte Funkzone

P

PABX (private automatic branch exchange)	Wählnebenstellenanlage
cordless ~	schnurlose Wählnebenstellenanlage
wireless ~	schnurlose Wählnebenstellenanlage
packet	Paket, Datenpaket
~ assembly	Paketierung
~ assembly/disassembly facility	Paketierer-/Depaketierer-Einrichtung
~ disassembly	Depaketierung
~ error probability	Paketfehlerwahrscheinlichkeit
~ format	Paketformat
~ mode	Paketbetrieb, Paketmodus
~ network	Paketnetz
~-oriented access procedure	paketorientierte Zugangsprozedur
~-oriented transmission of messages	paketweise Nachrichtenübermittlung
~ retransmission	Paketwiederholung
~-switched network	paketvermitteltes Netz
~ switching	Paketvermittlung
~-switching exchange	Paketvermittlungsamt
~-switching network	Paketvermittlungsnetz
~-switching procedure	Paketvermittlungsprozedur
~-terminal subscriber	Paketteilnehmer
page vb	jemanden ausrufen, rufen
page	Funkruf
answer vb a ~	Funkruf beantworten
pager	Funkrufempfänger, Anrufmelder
paging	Funkruf, Personenruf
~ area	Rufbereich
~ channel	Rufkanal
~ signal	Rufsignal

~ system	Personenrufanlage
~ terminal	Funkrufendgerät
alphanumeric ~	alphanumerischer Funkrufdienst
display ~	Funkruf mit Textanzeige, Funkrufdienst mit optischer Anzeige
off-site ~	öffentliches Funkrufsystem
on-site ~	privates Funkrufsystem
pan-European ~	europaweites Funkrufsystem
pan-European	europaweit
~ -European GSM standards	europaweite GSM-Standards
paper-free office	papierloses Büro
paperless office	papierloses Büro
parabolic antenna	Parabolantenne
~ disk antenna	Rotationsparabolantenne
paraboloid of revolution	Rotationsparaboloid
parallel ringing	Parallelruf
parasitic emissions	parasitäre Aussendungen
parked call	geparkte Verbindung
parent exchange	Mutteramt
partially restricted extension	halbamtsberechtigte Nebenstelle
party	Teilnehmer
~ line	Gemeinschaftsleitung
called ~	gerufener Teilnehmer
calling ~	rufender Teilnehmer, Anrufer
calling ~ pays, CPP	rufender Teilnehmer zahlt
pass vb out of range	die Reichweite verlassen
password	Kennwort
path	Weg, Strecke, Pfad
ascending ~	aufsteigender Weg
descending ~	absteigender Weg
~ attenuation	Streckendämpfung
~ control	Pfadsteuerung
~ loss	Streckendämpfung
pattern of faults	Fehlererscheinungsbild
pause signal control	Pausenzeichensteuerung
payphone	Münzer, Münzfernsprecher

paystation	Münzer, Münzfernsprecher
PBX line group	Sammelanschluß
voice/data ~	Sprach- und Daten-Nebenstellenanlage
PCM-30 time division multiplex system	PCM-30-Zeitmultiplexsystem
PCN (personal communication network)	individuelle mobile Kommunikation
peak air time	Hauptsendezeit
~ hour	Hauptverkehrsstunde
~ hours	Spitzenbelastungszeit
~ load	Spitzenbelastung
~ traffic	Spitzenverkehr
~ traffic mode	Stoßbetrieb
~ traffic period	Stoßzeit
period of ~ activity	Stoßzeit
peg count	Messung der Anzahl der Belegungsversuche, Messung der Belegungszahlen
peripheral event	Anreiz aus der Peripherie
~ switching equipment	vermittlungstechnische Peripherie
periphery	Peripherie
call-processing ~	vermittlungstechnische Peripherie
switching-oriented ~	vermittlungstechnische Peripherie
permanent circuit connection	Festnetzverbindung
~ connection	Festverbindung
international ~ circuit connection	internationale Festverbindung
terrestrial ~ circuit connection	terrestrische Festverbindung
~ virtual circuit	feste virtuelle Verbindung
personal authorization	personenbezogene Berechtigung
~ data	personenbezogene Daten
~ identification number, PIN	persönliche Kennummer
~ call number	persönliche Rufnummer
~ized call number	personenorientierte Rufnummer
~ized speed calling	individuelle Kurzwahl

phase averaging	Phasenmittlung
~ fading	Phasenschwund
~ jitter	Phasenjitter
~ modulation	Phasenmodulation
~ shift keying, PSK	Phasenumtastung
phone vb	anrufen
phone service	Telefondienst
cellular ~ service	zellularer Telefondienst
physical layer	Bitübertragungsschicht, physikalische Schicht
~ protocol	Bitübertragungsprotokoll
pigtail	Anschlußfaser (Lichtwellenleiter)
pilot receiver	Pilotempfänger
~ tone	Pilotton
point-to-point connection	Punktverbindung
~ -to-multipoint ISDN connection	Punkt-zu-Mehrpunkt-ISDN-Verbindung
pointing error (antenna)	Ausrichtfehler
polarization diversity	Polarisationsdiversity
polling	Abfrage, Abruf, Sendeabruf
~ phase	Aufforderungsphase zum Empfangen
~ signal	Datenabfragesignal
pool capacity utilized	Poolbelegung
poor transmission	schlechte Verständigung
population coverage	Versorgung der Bevölkerung (mit Diensten)
port	Zugangspunkt
portable adj	tragbar
~ cell site	transportable Basisstation, transportable Funkfeststation
~ coverage	Versorgung mit tragbaren Funktelefonen
~ mobile station	tragbare Mobilstation
~ radiotelephone	tragbares Mobiltelefon
~ subscriber	Teilnehmer mit tragbarem Mobiltelefon
position locating	Standortbestimmung
positive acknowledgement, ACK	positive Quittierung, positive Rückmeldung

power control	Netzausfallüberwachung, Leistungsregelung
~ control message	Netzausfallüberwachungsmeldung
~ delay profile	Verzögerungs-Leistungsspektrum
~ level	Leistungspegel
~ -up mode	Betriebszustand
precedence indicator	Prioritätsanzeige
~ signal	Dringlichkeitskennzeichen
prefix	Kennziffer
~ number	Vorwahlkennziffer
international ~	internationale Zugangskennzahl
presence signal	Anwesenheitszeichen
present vb	anbieten (z.B. Signal)
~ ed	abfragebereit (Wahlcode)
presentation	Darstellung, Anzeige
~ layer	Darstellungsschicht
~ protocol	Darstellungsprotokoll
calling line identification ~	Anzeige der Nummer des rufenden Teilnehmers
connected line identification ~	Anzeige der Nummer des gerufenen Teilnehmers
connected number identification ~ , ConNIP	Anzeige der gerufenen Nummer
press vb	drücken (Taste)
primary exchange	Hauptvermittlungsstelle
~ route	Direktweg, Erstweg
~ trunk group	Direktbündel
priority	Bevorrechtigung
~ access	vorrangiger Zugang
~ call	Vorrangverbindung
~ caller	bevorrechtigter Anrufer
~ connection	Vorrangverbindung
~ exchange	Prioritätenaustausch
outgoing/incoming ~	Priorität für abgehende/ankommende Rufe
privacy of personal data	Datenschutz
~ of telecommunications	Fernmeldegeheimnis

private automatic branch exchange, PABX	private Nebenstellenanlage
~ branch exchange, PBX	private Nebenstellenanlage
~ digital exchange, PDX	private digitale Nebenstellenanlage
~ telephone network	privates Fernsprechnetz
~ telephone operator	private Fernmeldegesellschaft
privileged operation	privilegierter Betrieb
probability of failure	Ausfallwahrscheinlichkeit
~ of loss	Verlustwahrscheinlichkeit
procedure	Prozedur, Ablauf, Verfahren
~ error	Ablauffehler
~ interface	Prozedurschnittstelle
invoked ~	aufgerufene Prozedur
invoking ~	aufrufende Prozedur
local ~ error	örtlicher Ablauffehler
proceed-to-select signal	Wahlaufforderungszeichen
~ -to-send signal	Abrufzeichen, Amtszeichen, Sendefreigabesignal
programming language	Programmiersprache
switching-oriented ~ language	vermittlungstechnisch orientierte Programmiersprache
progress message	Zwischenmeldung
prompter	Wecker
prompting	Bedienerführung
voice ~	akustische Bedienerführung
prompts	Bedienerführung
propagation	Ausbreitung (Wellen, Licht)
~ delay	Ausbreitungsverzögerung
~ forecast	Ausbreitungsvorhersage
~ loss	Ausbreitungsverlust
~ measurement	Ausbreitungsmessung
~ model	Ausbreitungsmodell
~ path	Ausbreitungsweg
~ prediction	Ausbreitungsvorhersage
~ rate	Ausbreitungsgeschwindigkeit
speed of ~	Ausbreitungsgeschwindigkeit

protection margin	Schutzreserve
~ ratio (against noise)	Schutzabstand
protocol	Protokoll
higher-level ~	höheres Protokoll
~ architecture	Protokollarchitektur
~ converter	Protokollwandler
~ layer	Protokollebene, Protokollschicht
~ standard	Protokollnorm
provide vb coverage (to a cell)	(eine Funkzone) versorgen
provider (services)	Anbieter (Dienste)
provision	Bereitstellung
public data network	öffentliches Datennetz
~ data transmission service	öffentlicher Datenübermittlungsdienst
~ land mobile network, PLMN	öffentliches bewegliches Landfunknetz, öffentliches Mobilfunknetz
~ land mobile service, PLMS	öffentlicher beweglicher Landfunkdienst, öffentlicher Mobilfunkdienst
~ leased-cirucit data network	öffentliches Direktrufnetz
~ mobile radio network	öffentliches bewegliches Landfunknetz
~ mobile telephone service	öffentlicher beweglicher Landfunkdienst
~ radio telephone service	öffentlicher beweglicher Landfunkdienst
~ recorded information service	Fernsprechansagedienst
~ switched network	öffentliches Vermittlungsnetz, öffentliches Wählnetz
~ switched telephone network, PSTN	öffentliches Selbstwählferndienstnetz, öffentliches Fernsprechnetz
~ telephone exchange	öffentliches Fernsprechamt
~ telephone operator	öffentliche Fernmeldegesellschaft
~ telephone network	öffentliches Fernsprechnetz
pulse amplitude modulation, PAM	Pulsamplitudenmodulation
~ code modulation, PCM	Pulscodemodulation
~ decay time	Abfallzeit (Impuls)
~ fall time	Abfallzeit (Impuls)
~ frequency modulation, PFM	Pulsfrequenzmodulation
~ phase modulation, PPM	Pulsphasenmodulation

~ signalling   Impulswahl
~ time modulation   Pulszeitmodulation
pulsing   Impulsgabe
pushbutton dialling   Tastenwahl
~ dialling telephone   Tastenfernsprecher
~ phone   Tastwahlapparat
~ selection   Tastenwahl
~ set   Fernsprechapparat mit Tastenwahl,
                                      Telefonapparat mit Wähltastatur
~ telephone   Tastenfernsprecher
push-to-talk button   Sprechtaste

quadrature phase shift keying,   Vierphasenumtastung
   QPSK
quality of service   Verkehrsgüte
~ -of-service meter   Gütezähler
   service ~   Dienstgüte
quantization   Quantisierung
~ distortion   Quantisierungsgeräusch
~ noise   Quantisierungsgeräusch
quantizing   Quantisierung
~ interval   Quantisierungsintervall
quasi-smooth terrain   quasiebenes Gelände
queue   Warteschlange
queuing   Warteschlangenbetrieb
~ condition   Wartestellung
~ operation   Warteverkehr
~ probability   Wartewahrscheinlichkeit
~ system   Wartesystem

quick test   Geradeaustest
quota-based allocation of traffic   Quotieren
~ -based distribution of traffic   Quotieren
    call ~ allocation table   Quotierungstabelle

R

radially, connect vb ~   sternförmig verbinden
radiate vb (power)   abstrahlen (Leistung)
radiated power   abgestrahlte Leistung, Strahlungs-
                                        leistung
    effective ~ power   äquivalente Strahlungsleistung
radio amateur   Amateurfunker
~ -based mobile phone service   Mobilfunkdienst
~ carrier frequency   Funkträgerfrequenz
~ cell   Funkzone
~ channel   Funkkanal
~ channel group   Frequenzkanalbündel
~ communication   Funkverkehr
~ congestion   Funküberlastung
~ contact   Funkverbindung
~ control   Funkfernsteuerung
~ control station   Leitfunkstelle
~ coverage   Funkversorgung, Funkbedeckung,
                                        Reichweite
~ coverage area   Funkversorgungsgebiet
~ data transmission   Datenfunk
~ detector van   Funkpeilfahrzeug
~ environment   Funkumfeld
~ frequency   Funkfrequenz
~ frequency channel, RF channel   Hochfrequenzkanal, HF-Kanal
~ horizon   Funkhorizont

~ interface	Luftschnittstelle
~ interference	Funkstörung
~ interference level	Funkstörgrad
~ link	Funkverbindung, Richtfunkstrecke
~ link hop	Funkfeld
~ location network	Funkortungsnetz
~ location service	Funkortungsdienst
~ network	Funknetz
cellular ~ network	zellulares Funknetz
~ network design	Funknetzentwurf
~ noise voltage	Funkstörspannung
~ paging	Funkruf
~ paging service	Funkrufdienst
~ paging system	Funkrufdienst
European ~ paging system	europäischer Funkrufdienst, Euro-Signal
~ path	Funkweg
~ receiver	Funkempfänger
~ reception	Funkempfang
~ regulations, RR	Vollzugsordnung für den Funkdienst
~ relay system	Richtfunk
~ service	Funkdienst
~ signal	Funksignal
~ station	Funkstelle
~ subscriber	Funkteilnehmer
cellular ~ system	zellulares Funksystem
~ telegraphy	drahtlose Telegrafie
~ telephone	Funktelefon
~ telephone network	Funkfernsprechnetz
~ telephone service	Funktelefondienst
~ telephone system	Funkfernsprechsystem
~ telephony	Funkfernsprechen, Sprechfunk
~ tower	Fernmeldeturm
~ traffic	Funkverkehr
~ transmission	Funkübertragung, drahtlose Übertragung
~ transmitter	Funksender
~ wave damping	Funkfelddämpfung
~ waves	Funkwellen
~ zone	Funkzone
loss of ~ contact	Abreißen der Funkverbindung

radome	Antennenkuppel, Radom
raised-cosine pulse	Kosinusquadrat-Impuls
ramp time	Anstiegszeit (Impuls)
random access channel, RACH	Direktzugriffkanal
~ frequency modulation	stochastische Frequenzmodulation, ausbreitungsbedingte Frequenzmodulation
range	Reichweite
switching ~	vermittlungstechnische Reichweite
pass vb out of ~	die Reichweite verlassen
rate	Gebühr, Tarif
flat rate	Pauschaltarif
Rayleigh criterion	Rayleigh-Kriterium
~ distribution	Rayleigh-Verteilung
~ fading	Rayleigh-Schwund, Kurzzeitschwund
ready condition	Bereitzustand
~ state	Bereitzustand
~ to operate	betriebsbereit
~ to receive	empfangsbereit
~ -to-receive state	Empfangsbereitschaft
reattempt	Anrufwiederholung
~ on busy	Neuversuch bei Besetztzustand
recall vb	abrufen
recall(ing)	Abruf
receipt confirmation	Empfangsbestätigung
receive acknowledgement	Empfangsquittung, Empfangsbestätigung
~ buffer	Empfangspuffer
~ mode	Empfangsbetrieb
~ pause	Empfangspause
~ ready	empfangsbereit
receiver	Empfänger, Hörer
~ antenna	Empfängerantenne
~ inset	Hörkapsel
~ threshold	Empfängerschwellwert
receiving antenna	Empfangsantenne

~ end	Empfängerseite
~ land station	ortsfeste Empfangsfunkstelle
reception	Empfang
~ confirmation signal	Empfangsbestätigung
~ quality	Empfangsqualität, Empfangsgüte
unattended ~ (facsimile)	automatischer Empfang
reconfiguration	Konfigurationsänderung, Rekonfiguration
reconstructed sample	zurückgebildeter Abtastwert
recorded announcement service	Ansagedienst
recording	Aufzeichnung
DC bias ~	Aufzeichnung mit Gleichstromvormagnetisierung
non-return-to-reference ~	Aufzeichnung ohne Rückkehr zum Bezugszustand
return-to-reference ~	Aufzeichnung mit Rückkehr zum Bezugszustand
return-to-zero ~	Aufzeichnung mit Rückkehr nach Null
recover vb (error)	(Fehler) beheben
recovery	Wiederherstellung
redirection	Umleitung
redundancy	Redundanz
~ check	Redundanzprüfung
redundant routing	Mehrwegeführung
refer-back facility	Rückfrageeinrichtung
reference clock pulse	Bezugtakt
~ frequency	Bezugsfrequenz
reflection	Reflexion
~ coefficient	Reflexionsfaktor
refraction	Brechung (Lichtwellenleiter)
index of ~	Brechungskoeffizient
refractive index	Brechungskoeffizient
~ index profile	Brechzahlprofil
reframing	Rahmenwiederherstellung
refresh alarm	Auffrischalarm

regional switch	Hauptvermittlungsstelle
register vb	einbuchen
registration	Einbuchung
location ~	Einbuchen in die Standortdatei
regular routing	Regelverkehr
relative distance measurement	relative Entfernungsmessung
relay switching matrix	Relaiskoppelfeld
release vb	freigeben, freischalten
reliability and failure analysis	Zuverlässigkeits- und Ausfallanalyse
remedy vb (defect)	(Fehler, Mangel) beheben
reminder signal	Erinnerungssignal
remote	abgesetzt (Endgerät)
~ control technology	Fernwirktechnik
~ diagnosis	Ferndiagnose
~ reading (of meters)	Fernablesen (von Zählern)
remove vb (fault)	(Fehler) beseitigen
rental	Mietgebühr
repeated call attempt	wiederholter Verbindungsversuch
repeater	Verstärker
~ satellite	Relaissatellit
repetitive error	wiederholt auftretender Fehler
replace vb (A by B)	austauschen, ersetzen
~ (receiver)	auflegen (Hörer)
request	Anforderung, Aufforderung
~ for operator service	Platzanforderung
~ for repeat	Wiederholungsanforderung
~ lockout	Anforderungssperre
central ~ lockout	zentrale Anforderungssperre
program ~	Programmanforderung
re-ring vb	Ruf wiederholen
re-ringing	Nachrufen
~-ringing signal	Nachrufzeichen
rerouting	Umleitung

reset vb	rücksetzen, zurücksetzen, zurückstellen
~ collision	Rücksetzzusammenstoß
residual traffic	Restverkehr
resonating reflector	Resonanzreflektor
restoral attempt	Wiedereinschaltversuch
restoration	Wiederherstellung
restricted night service	Nachtkonzentration
restriction	Unterdrückung
calling line identification ~	Unterdrückung der Anzeige der Nummer des rufenden Teilnehmers
connected line identification ~	Unterdrückung der Anzeige der Nummer des gerufenen Teilnehmers
retrieval	Abruf
retrieve vb	abrufen
~ /copy from memory	Abrufen/Kopieren aus dem Speicher
retry	Rufwiederholung, wiederholter Versuch
automatic ~	automatische Rufwiederholung
return to service	Wiederinbetriebnahme
~ -to-zero code	RZ-Code, Rückkehr nach Null-Code
reuse	Wiederholung
~ distance	Wiederholabstand
revenue call	gebührenpflichtiger Anruf
reverse vb polarity	umpolen
reverse charging	R-Gespräch
~ charging request	Anforderung der Gebührenübernahme
~ charging acceptance	Annahme der Gebührenübernahme, Zustimmung zur Gebührenübernahme
~ d charging	Gebührenübernahme
RF channel, radio frequency channel	Hochfrequenzkanal, HF-Kanal
~ protection ratio	HF-Schutzabstand, hochfrequenter Schutzabstand
~ signal-to-interference ratio	HF-Störabstand
ridged waveguide	Steghohlleiter

right-of-access code	Berechtigungszeichen
ring vb	rufen, klingeln
~ up vb	anrufen
ring back vb	zurückrufen
ring configuration	Ringstruktur
~ pause	Rufpause
~ network	Ringnetz
~ topology	Ringtopologie
ringback	Nachrufen, Rückruf
~ acknowledgement	Freizeichenquittung
~ signal	Nachrufzeichen, Verbunden-Signal
~ tone	Rufton (rückwärts)
ringer	Klingel
ringing length	Meldewartezeit
~ queue	Rufwarteschlange
~ signal	Rufsignal, Rufzeichen
~ tone	Rufton (vorwärts), Freiton
road fax	Auto-Telefaxgerät
roamer clearing house	Roamer-Verrechnungsstelle
roaming	Roaming, Wandern (freier Rufbereichswechsel)
~ indication	Umbuchnachricht
mobile station ~ number, MSRN	Roaming-Nummer
national ~	nationales Roaming
rod antenna	Stabantenne
roof-top antenna	Dachantenne
roundtrip delay	Hin- und Rückwegverzögerung
route vb	leiten, weiterleiten
route	Leitweg, Strecke
~ alarm	Streckenalarm
~ channel	Streckenkanal
~ clock pulse	Streckentakt
~ congestion	Streckenüberlastung
~ discriminating digit	Richtungsausscheidungsziffer
~ diversion	Umlenkung

~ selector	Richtungswähler
~ section	Streckenabschnitt
final ~	Letztweg
routing	Leitweglenkung, Verkehrslenkung
~ command	Leitbefehl
~ control	Leitwegsteuerung
~ information	Leitinformationen
adaptive ~	adaptive Verkehrslenkung
diverse ~	Umleitung
fixed ~	feste Verkehrslenkung
redundant ~	Mehrwegeführung, Vermaschung
rural areas	ländliche Gebiete
~ exchange	Landzentrale

S

safety from interception	Abhörsicherheit
sample vb	(Signale, Impulse) abtasten
sample	Abtastwert
reconstructed ~	zurückgebildeter Abtastwert
sampling	Abtastung
~ distortion	Abtastverzerrung
~ instant	Abtastzeitpunkt
~ theorem	Abtasttheorem
~ time-slot pattern	Abtastzeitraster
satellite	Satellit
~ communication	Satellitenfunk, Satellitenkommunikation
~ earth station	Satelliten-Erdfunkstelle
~ exchange	Satellitenamt
~ link	Satellitenstrecke

mobile ~ services	mobile Satellitendienste
~ transmission	Satellitenübertragung
direct broadcasting ~	direktstrahlender Satellit
geostationary ~	geostatinärer Satellit
scan vb	(Signale, Impulse) abtasten
scanning	Abtastung
~ speed	Abtastgeschwindigkeit
scatterer	Streuer
scattering	Streuung
scrambler	Scrambler, Verwürfler
scrambling	Verwürfelung
screenmail	Bildschirmpost
search with homing	Suchverfahren mit Nullstellung
seatphone	Telefonapparat pro Sitzreihe (im Flugzeug)
secondary route	Zweitweg
secrecy of telecommunications	Fernmeldegeheimnis
section-by-section transmission	abschnittsweise Übertragung
sector	Sektor
~ antenna	Sektorantenne
~ ized antenna	Sektorantenne
~ cell	Sektorzelle
~ operation	Sektorbetrieb
~ reuse	Sektorwiederholung
security against tapping	Abhörsicherheit
segment vb	segmentieren
seize vb (a line)	(Leitung) belegen
seized adj	belegt
seizure	Belegung
~ command	Belegungsbefehl
incoming ~	kommende Belegung
outgoing ~	gehende Belegung
select vb	ansteuern, (mit Tastatur) wählen, anwählen

selection code presented	Wahlcode abfragebereit
selective call	selektiver Anruf, Selektivruf
selectivity	Selektivität, Trennschärfe
adjacent-channel ~	Trennschärfe gegen den Nachbarkanal
self-location	automatische Standorterfassung
~-supporting mast	freitragender Antennenmast
~-test software	Eigentest-Software
semirigid waveguide	biegbarer Hohlleiter
send vb (messages)	(Meldungen) ausgeben
sequence	Ablauf
~ and refresh control	Ablauf- und Refresh-Steuerung
call-processing ~	vermittlungstechnischer Ablauf
user-related ~	teilnehmerbezogener Ablauf
serial transmission	serielle Übertragung
serve vb calls	Verbindungen abwickeln
~ subscribers	Teilnehmer bedienen, versorgen, betreuen
server	Server
~ common control	Server-Zentralsteuerung
adapted ~	adaptierter Server
service vb	(Unterbrechungen) abarbeiten
service	Betrieb, Dienst
~ access code	Funknetzkennzahl
~ area	Bedienungsbereich, Betriebsbereich, Versorgungsbereich, Versorgungsgebiet, Funkverkehrsbereich, Reichweite, Dienstbereich, Netzbreich
~ attribute	Dienstattribut
~ category	Dienstart
basic ~s	Grunddienste
~ code	Funknetzkennzahl
~ feature	Dienstmerkmal
demand ~	Sofortverkehr
enhanced ~s	erweiterte Dienste, Zusatzdienste
higher-level ~s	höhere Dienste
grade of ~	Dienstgüte
in ~	in Betrieb

    integrated ~s digital network, ISDN   diensteintegrierendes digitales Netz
    mobile telephone ~   Mobilfunkdienst, Funksprechdienst
    out of ~   außer Betrieb
    special ~   Sonderdienst
    standard ~s   Grunddienste, Standarddienste
    supplementary ~s   Zusatzdienste
    switched ~s   leitungsvermittelte Dienste
    value-added ~s   Mehrwertdienste
~ attribute   Dienstmerkmal
~ coverage   Diensteversorgung
~ enhancement   Diensterweiterung
~ feature   Dienstmerkmal
~ integration   Diensteintegration
~ interworking   Dienstübergang
~ mix   Dienstespektrum
~ probability   Versorgungswahrscheinlichkeit
~ provider   Diensteanbieter, Dienstebringer
~ provision   Diensteangebot
~ quality   Dienstgüte
~ signal   Dienstsignal
~ -specific network   dienstspezifisches Netz
    mobile telphone ~   Mobilfunkdienst, Funksprechdienst
~ traffic   Dienstverkehr
~ user   Dienstteilnehmer
~ 130   Service 130
serving base station   betreuende Basisstation, versorgende Basisstation, betreuende Funkfeststation
~ channel   Abnehmerkanal
~ line   Abnehmer, Abnehmerleitung, Partnerleitung
~ port   Partnerleitung
~ port address   Abnehmeradresse
~ time   Abwicklungszeit
~ trunk   Abnehmer, Abnehmerleitung
~ trunk group   Abnehmerbündel
session layer   Sitzungsschicht
~ layer management   Sitzungsschicht-Verwaltung

set up vb (connection, call)	aufbauen, herstellen (Verbindung)
setup (call)	Aufbau (Verbindung)
~ up time	Verbindungsherstellzeit
off-air call ~	sprechkanalfreier Verbindungsaufbau, Verbindungsaufbau ohne Sprechkanalbelegung
seven-layer model	7-Schichtenmodell
shaded area	Schattenzone
shadow area	Schattenzone
~ fading	langsamer Schwund
~ ing	Abschattung
share vb	mitbenutzen
shared service line	Gemeinschaftsleitung
shift key	Umschalttaste
~ keying	Umtastung (Modulation)
ship-to-shore radio	Seefunkdienst
short dialling	Kurzwahl
~ -distance traffic	Nahverkehr
~ -haul traffic	Nahverkehr
~ message	Kurznachricht, Kurztelegramm
~ message service	Kurzmitteilungsdienst
~ occupation	Kurzbelegung
~ -range radio	Kurzwellenfunk
~ -term fading	Kurzzeitschwund, Rayleigh-Schwund
~ -term filing	Kurzzeitarchivierung
~ -term median	Kurzzeitmedianwert
~ -text announcer	Hinweis-Ansagegerät
~ -time storage	Kurzspeicher
sidetone	Nebenton, Rückhörgeräusch
~ suppression	Rückhördämpfung
signal vb	Zeichen geben
signal	Signal
~ buffer	Zeichenpuffer
~ converter	Signalumsetzer, Signalwandler
~ element length	Schrittdauer
~ level	Feldstärkepegel, Signalpegel
~ processor	Signalprozessor

digital ~ processing	digitale Signalverarbeitung
~ propagation time	Signallaufzeit
~ strength	Nutzfeldstärke
~ suppression noise	Signalunterdrückungsrauschen
~-to-crosstalk ratio	Signal-Nebensprechverhältnis
~-to-interference ratio, S/I ratio, SIR	Störabstand, Signal-Störleistungsverhältnis
~-to-noise ratio	Geräuschabstand, Rauschabstand, Signal-Geräuschabstand, Störabstand, Signal-Rauschabstand, Signal-Rauschleistungsverhältnis
~ wraparound	Informationsumkehr
ringback ~	Freizeichen
start-dialling ~	Wahlbereitzeichen, Amtszeichen
status ~	Meldung
unwanted ~	ungewünschtes Signal
wanted ~	gewünschtes Signal
signalling	Signalisierung, Signalgabe, Zeichengabe
~ channel	Zeichengabekanal
~ information	Zeichengabeinformationen
~ link	Zeichengabeabschnitt
~ link terminal	Endeinrichtung für den zentralen Zeichengabekanal
~ link transceiver	Sende-/Empfangseinrichtung für den zentralen Zeichengabekanal
~ network	Zeichengabenetz
~ pattern	Raster
~ protocol	Zeichengabeprotokoll
~ rate	Schrittgeschwindigkeit
~ reliability	Zuverlässigkeit der Zeichengabe
~ speed (bits/s)	Übertragungsgeschwindigkeit
~ system No. 7 (SS #7)	Zeichengabesystem Nr. 7
~ traffic	Zeichengabeverkehr
associated ~	assoziierte Zeichengabe
channel-associated ~	kanalgebundene Zeichengabe
common-channel ~	Zeichengabe mit gemeinsamem Zeichenkanal
link-by-link ~	abschnittsweise Zeichengabe
multi-frequency ~	Mehrfrequenzzeichengabe

user-to-user ~ , UUS	Teilnehmer-Teilnehmer-Zeichengabe
visual ~	optische Signalisierung
sign off vb	abmelden
sign-off	Abmeldung
~ -off request	Abmeldeanforderung
sign on vb	anmelden, einbuchen
sign-on	Anmeldung
~ -on request	Anmeldeanforderung
silence	Funkstille
impose vb ~	Funkstille auferlegen
zone of ~	tote Zone
silent zone	tote Zone
silica-glass fiber	Quarzglasfaser (Lichtwellenleiter)
simplex	Simplex, Wechselsprechen
~ mode	Simplex-Betrieb, Einwegbetrieb
simultaneous transmission	simultane Übertragung
single-channel through-connection	Einzelkanal-Durchschaltung
~ -character call forward mode	Einzelabrufbetrieb
~ clock pulse	Einzeltakt
~ mode fiber	Einmodenfaser, Monomodefaser
~ sideband amplitude modulation	Einseitenband-Amplitudenmodulation
~ -mode fiber	Einmodenfaser, Monomodefaser
site	Standort
~ diversity	Standortdiversity
~ search	vorausgehende Standortklärung
siting	Standortwahl
skyphone (British Telecom)	Telefonservice für Flugzeugpassagiere
small cell	Kleinzone
~ radio cell	Kleinzelle
~ radio zone	Kleinzelle
smart card	Chipkarte
~ card reader	Chipkartenleser
~ interface	intelligente Schnittstelle

smoothing circuit	Abflachschaltung
Sn bits	Zeichengabebits
Snell's law	Brechungsgesetz
softkey	Softtaste
software	Software
~ provider	Softwareanbieter (z.B. Btx)
call processing ~	vermittlungstechnische Software
dependability ~	Sicherungssoftware
dependability system ~	sicherheitstechnische Software
loadable ~	ladbare Software
solid-state matrix	Festkörperkoppler
space diversity	Raumdiversity
~-division multiplex connection	Raumvielfachverbindung
~-division multiplex method	Raummultiplexverfahren
spatial traffic demand	räumliches Verkehrsaufkommen
spectral efficiency	Frequenzökonomie
~ frequency	Spektralfrequenz
~ power density	Leistungsdichtespektrum
spectrum efficiency	Frequenzökonomie
speech	Sprache
~ band	Sprachband (Frequenzen)
~ circuit	Sprechkreis
~ connection with accompanying text transmission	textbegleitende Sprechverbindung
~ /data channel	Nutzkanal
~ deviation	Frequenzhub (Sprache)
~ processing	Sprachverarbeitung
~ scrambler	Sprachverwürfler
~ scrambling	Sprachverschleierung
~ signal	Sprachsignal
~ transmission	Sprachübertragung
digitize vb ~	Sprache digitalisieren
speed calling with name keys	Zielwahl mit Namenstasten
~ dialling	Kurzwahl
~ dialling code	Kurzrufnummer
name key for ~ dialling	Namenstaste für Kurzwahl

personalized ~ dialling | individuelle Kurzwahl
~ of propagation | Ausbreitungsgeschwindigkeit
spreading loss | Streudämpfung
spurious emissions | Nebenaussendungen
standby channel | Ersatzkanal
~ mode | Reserve-Betriebsart
~ service | Bereitschaftsbetrieb
star configuration | Sternkonfiguration
~ network | Sternstruktur
start-dialling signal | Amtszeichen, Wahlbereitzeichen
~ of ringing | Freizeichen
~ -of-text character, STX character | Anfangszeichen
~ -stop distortion | Start-/Stopp-Verzerrung
~ -stop system | Start-/Stopp-Verfahren
~ -up peak | Einschaltspitze
~ -up phase | Anlaufphase
static-picture transmission | Standbildübertragung
station | Teilnehmerstation, Teilnehmer
~ forced busy | Anrufschutz
~ guarding | Anrufschutz
stationary | ortsfest
~ user | stationärer Teilnehmer
status indication | Betriebszustandsanzeige
~ inquiry signal | Zustandsabfragesignal
~ message | Meldung
~ request | Statusabfrage
~ signal | Meldung
steep-sloped (signal) | steil (Signal)
step index fiber | Stufenprofilfaser
~ index optical waveguide | Stufenprofilfaser
~ index profile | Stufenprofil
still image | Stehbild
~ picture communication | Festbildkommunikation
stolen vehicle locator service | Ortungsdienst für gestohlene Fahrzeuge

store-and-forward mode	Speicherbetrieb
~ -and-forward service	Speicherdienst, Speicher- und Verarbeitungsdienst
~ -and-forward switching	Speichervermittlung
~ -and-forward switching center	Speichervermittlungsstelle
stored-program adj	speicherprogrammiert
~ -program control	speicherprogrammierte Steuerung
~ -program electronic switch	speicherprogrammierte elektronische Vermittlungsstelle
automatic ~ -program switching center	speicherprogrammierte Wählvermittlung
straight-forward test	Geradeaustest
subband coding, SBC	Teilbandcodierung
subcarrier modulation	Hilfsträgermodulation, Zwischenträgermodulation
subchannel	Unterkanal
submarine cable	Ozeankabel, Seekabel
subscriber	Teilnehmer
~ authentication key	Teilnehmerautorisierungsschlüssel
~ base	Teilnehmerkreis
~ behaviour	Teilnehmerverhalten
~ capacity	Teilnehmerkapazität
~ class	Teilnehmerklasse
~ data	Teilnehmerdaten
~ database	Teilnehmerdatenbank
~ -dialled call	Selbstwählverbindung
~ equipment	Teilnehmergeräte
~ identification	Teilnehmerkennung
~ identity module	Teilnehmerkennungsmodul
~ information	Teilnehmerdaten
~ line	Teilnehmeranschluß
~ 's number	Rufnummer
~ 's rental	Grundgebühr
~ set	Teilnehmerapparat
~ trunk dialling, STD	Selbstwählfernverkehr, Fernwahl
~ unit	Teilnehmergerät
~ usage pattern	Teilnehmernutzungsverhalten
busy vb out a ~	Sperren eines Teilnehmers

called ~	gerufener Teilnehmer
calling ~	rufender Teilnehmer
cellular ~	Teilnehmer am zellularen Mobilfunk
directory of ~ s	Teilnehmerverzeichnis
local ~	Ortsteilnehmer, Ortsnetzteilnehmer
mobile ~	mobiler Teilnehmer
temporary mobile ~ identity	zeitweilige Teilnehmerkennung
substitute vb (B for A)	ersetzen, austauschen
suburban traffic	Vorortverkehr
successful call	erfolgreich abgewickelter Anruf, erfolgreiche Belegung
successor signal	Folgesignal
suffix dialling	Nachwahl
supervisory tone	Überwachungston
supplementary services	Zusatzdienste
support vb (e.g. a procedure)	(Verfahren) unterstützen
suppress vb interference	entstören
surface wave filter	Oberflächenwellenfilter
suspended event	wartender Anreiz
switch vb	vermitteln
switch	Vermittlungsstelle
digital ~	digitale Vermittlungsstelle
stored-program electronic ~	speicherprogrammierte elektronische Vermittlungsstelle
switched connection	leitungsvermittelte Verbindung Wählverbindung
~ data traffic	Datenwählverkehr
~ network	leitungsvermitteltes Netz
~ services	leitungsvermittelte Dienste
~ telephone network	Fernsprechwählnetz
~ virtual circuit	gewählte virtuelle Verbindung
switching	Vermittlung
automatic stored-program ~ center	speicherprogrammierte Wählvermittlung
~ diversity	Schaltdiversity
~ information	Leitinformationen

~ matrix   Koppelvielfach, Koppelmatrix
~ matrix for dedicated lines   Standleitungskoppler
~ network   Koppelfeld, Koppelnetzwerk, Koppelnetz
~ node   Vermittlungsknoten
~ -oriented macro language   vermittlungstechnische Makrosprache
~ -oriented periphery   vermittlungstechnische Peripherie
~ -oriented programming language   vermittlungstechnisch orientierte Programmiersprache
~ processor   Vermittlungsrechner
~ range   vermittlungstechnische Reichweite
~ signal   Schaltkennzeichen
~ system processor   Steuerrechner für Vermittlungssysteme

  circuit ~   Leitungsvermittlung
  mobile ~ center, MSC   Mobilvermittlungsstelle, Überleiteinrichtung

  mobile services ~ center   Mobilvermittlungsstelle, Überleiteinrichtung

  non-blocking ~ network   blockierungsfreies Koppelfeld
  peripheral ~ equipment   vermittlungstechnische Peripherie
  semi-automatic ~   halbautomatische Vermittlung

switch off vb   abschalten (z.B. Gerät)

synchronized network   Synchronnetz

synchronism, work vb in ~   synchron arbeiten

synchronization control   Gleichlaufsteuerung
~ information   Synchronisierinformationen
~ procedure   Gleichlaufverfahren

synchronizing signal   Synchronisationszeichen

synchronous mode   Synchronbetrieb
~ transmission   synchrone Übertragung

system access   Systemanschaltung, Systemzugang
~ affiliation   Systemzugehörigkeit
~ area   Netzbereich
~ breakdown   Systemausfall
~ collapse   Netzzusammenbruch
~ failure   Systemausfall
~ features   Systemmerkmale

~ loss Funkfelddämpfung
~ startup Systemhochlauf
~ status control Systemzustandssteuerung

T

table telephone Tischapparat
tabletop facsimile equipment Tischfernkopierer
TACS (Total Access Communication System) TACS (britisches Mobilfunksystem)
take off vb (handset) abnehmen, abheben (Hörer)
talk-back loudspeaker Mikrofonlautsprecher
tandem Durchgangsvermittlungsstelle
~ access Tandemzugriff
~ switching Transitvermittlung
~ switching center Durchgangsvermittlungsstelle
tariff Tarif
~ zone Tarifzone
telecommunications equipment Fernmeldeanlagen, Fernmeldeeinrichtungen
~ infrastructure Fernmelde-Infrastruktur
~ installations Fernmeldeanlagen
~ network Fernmeldenetz
~ office Fernmeldeamt
~ operator Fernmeldegesellschaft
~ services Fernmeldedienste
~ technology Nachrichtentechnik
  privacy of ~ Fernmeldegeheimnis
  secrecy of ~ Fernmeldegeheimnis
teleconference Telekonferenz
  fixed-image ~ Festbild-Telekonferenz

telecontrol | Fernwirken
~ link | Fernwirkverbindung
~ network | Fernwirknetz
~ plant | Fernwirkanlage

telecopy vb | fernkopieren

telematics | Telematik

telemetering | Fernmessen, Telemetrie, Meßwert-Fernübertragung

telemetry | Fernmessen, Telemetrie, Meßwert-Fernübertragung

~ exchange | TEMEX (Fernwirk-, Fernmeß- und Fernüberwachungsdienst)

telephone | Telefon, Fernsprecher
~ answering set | Anrufbeantworter
~ conference | Telefonkonferenz, Konferenzgespräch, Audiokonferenz

~ directory | Telefonbuch, Fernsprechverzeichnis
electronic ~ directory | elektronisches Telefonbuch
~ network | Fernsprechnetz, Telefonnetz
~ traffic | Fernsprechverkehr, Telefonverkehr
intercontinental ~ traffic | interkontinentaler Fernsprechverkehr

analog ~ network | analoges Fernsprechnetz
automatic analog public ~ network | öffentliches analoges Fernsprechwählnetz
compact ~ | Kompakttelefon
dial-up ~ network | Fernsprechwählnetz
digital ~ network | digitales Fernsprechnetz
DDD coinbox ~ | Fernmünzer
general switched ~ network | öffentliches Fernsprechwählnetz
private ~ network | privates Fernsprechnetz
public mobile ~ network | öffentlicher beweglicher Landfunkdienst

public ~ network | öffentliches Fernsprechnetz
pushbutton (dialling) ~ | Tastenfernsprecher
switched ~ network | Fernsprechwählnetz
table ~ | Tischapparat
touch-tone ~ | Tastwahlapparat

teleprinter | Fernschreiber

teleservices	Teledienste
teleshopping terminal	Bestellterminal
teletype	Fernschreiber
teletex network	Teletexnetz
~ service	Teletexdienst
~ station	Teletex-Endgerät
~ subscriber	Teletexteilnehmer
~ terminal	Teletex-Endgerät
telex	Telex
~ and data network	Fernschreib- und Datennetz
~ network	Telexnetz
~ signalling unit	Telexfernschaltgerät
~ subscriber	Telexteilnehmer
~ terminal	Telexteilnehmergerät
~ terminal repeater	Telex-Anschaltgerät
temporary mobile subscriber identity, TMSI	zeitweilige Teilnehmerkennung
terminal	Terminal, Endgerät, Datenendgerät
~ computer	Endstellenrechner
~ equipment	Endgeräte, Endeinrichtungen
~ station	Datenstation (Datenendeinrichtung + Datenübertragungseinrichtung)
national ~ number	nationale Rufnummer
signalling link ~	Endeinrichtung für den zentralen Zeichengabekanal
teleshopping ~	Bestellterminal
terminate vb	abbrechen (Programm)
terminated adj, mobile-~	ankommend
terminating	ankommend
~ international exchange	Eingangs-Kopfvermittlungsstelle
terrain	Gelände
~ features	Geländemerkmale
~ type	Geländeformation
irregular ~	nicht quasiebenes Gelände
quasi-smooth ~	quasiebenes Gelände
terrestrial permanent circuit connection	terrestrische Festverbindung
~ radio system	Erdfunksystem

tertiary area	Zentralvermittlungsstellenbereich
test vb for continuity	auf Durchgang prüfen
testing trunk group	Prüfbündel
test line group	Prüfbündel
~ log	Testprotokoll
~ mobile	Testmobil
~ pattern	Prüfmuster
~ route	Versuchsstrecke
~ tone reference	Testtonreferenz
text and data network	Text- und Datennetz
integrated ~ and data network	integriertes Text- und Datennetz, IDN
three-party conference	Dreierkonferenz
~-party service	Drei-Teilnehmer-Gespräch
~-party services	Drei-Teilnehmer-Dienste
through-connected adj	durchgeschaltet
~-connection	Durchschaltung
throughput	Durchsatz
tie line	Querverbindungsleitung
~ trunk	Querverbindungsleitung
time vb	zeitlich festlegen, takten
~ out vb	ablaufen (Zeitgeber)
time	Zeit
~ and distance meter	Zeitzonenzähler
~ and zone meter	Zeitzonenzähler
~ diversity	Zeitdiversity
~-division multiplex	Zeitmultiplex
~-division multiplex access, TDMA	TDMA-Zugriffsverfahren, Vielfachzugriff im Zeitmultiplex, Zeitmultiplex-Vielfachzugriff
PCM-30 ~-division multiplex system	PCM-30-Zeitmultiplexsystem
~-division multiplexing	Zeitmultiplexverfahren
~-division multiplex network	Zeitmultiplex-Durchschaltenetz
~ domain equalizer	Zeitbereichsentzerrer
adaptive ~ domain equalizer	adaptiver Zeitbereichsentzerrer
~ frame	Zeitskala
~ hopping	Zeitsprungverfahren

~ metering	Zeitzählung
~ pulse	Zeittaktimpuls
~ slot	Zeitschlitz, Zeitintervall
active part of ~ slot	aktiver Teil des Zeitschlitzes
~-slot pattern	Zeitraster
busy ~	Belegungszeit
holding ~	Belegungszeit
occupancy ~	Belegungszeit
operate vb in a ~-division mode	im Zeitmultiplexbetrieb arbeiten
unavailable ~	nicht verfügbare Zeit
timing error	Rasterverzerrung
~ extraction	Taktableitung
~ pattern	Taktraster
~ pulse train	Mäanderfolge
token	Token
~-passing access	Token-Passing-Zugang
~ ring	Token-Ring (Netz)
toll center	Fernvermittlung
~ charges	Sprechgebühren
~ exchange	Fernamt
~-free	gebührenfrei
tone-only paging	Nur-Ton-Funkrufdienst
~ plus voice paging	Ton-plus-Stimme-Funkrufdienst
~ quality	Tonqualität
~ signal	Tonsignal
~ time slot	Hörtonzeitlage
inject vb a ~	einen Ton anlegen
topographical data	Geländedaten
~ structure	Höhenstruktur
topology	Topologie
total loss	Systemdämpfung
touch-tone set	Tastwahlapparat
tower antenna	Turmantenne
tracking	Lokalisierung, Verfolgung
~ system	Verfolgungssystem
automatic ~	automatische Lokalisierung
electronic ~	elektronische Verfolgung

traffic   Verkehr
~ analysis   Verkehrsauswertung, Verkehrsanalyse
~ carrying capacity   Verkehrsleistung
~ channel, TCH   Nachrichtenkanal, Verkehrskanal
~ congestion   Verkehrsstauung
~ count   Verkehrszählung
~ demand   Verkehrsaufkommen
  spatial ~ demand   räumliches Verkehrsaufkommen
~ density   Verkehrsdichte
~ distribution   Verkehrsaufteilung, Verkehrverteilung
~ growth   Verkehrszunahme
~ handling capacity   Verkehrskapazität, Leistungsfähigkeit

~ load   Verkehrslast, Verkehrsbelastung
  mean ~ load   mittlere Verkehrsbelastung
~ model   Verkehrsmodell
~ pattern   Verkehrsverhalten, Verkehrsverlauf
~ peak   Verkehrsspitze
~ routing   Leitweglenkung
~ simulation   Verkehrssimulation
  mean ~ carried   mittlere Verkehrsbelastung
~ unit   Gebühreneinheit
~ volume   Verkehrsaufkommen
  handle vb ~   Verkehr abwickeln
  inbound ~   ankommender Verkehr, kommender Verkehr

  incoming ~   ankommender Verkehr, kommender Verkehr

  intercontinental telephone ~   interkontinentaler Fernsprechverkehr
  local ~   Ortsverkehr
  offered ~   Verkehrsangebot
  outbound ~   abgehender Verkehr, gehender Verkehr

  outgoing ~   abgehender Verkehr, gehender Verkehr

  suburban ~   Vorortverkehr
  transit ~   Durchgangsverkehr
train radio   Zugfunk
~ telephone   Zugtelefon

transceiver	Sende-/Empfangseinrichtung
signalling link ~	Sende-/Empfangseinrichtung für den zentralen Zeichengabekanal
transfer in channel	Kanalsprung
~ time	Transferzeit
cross-office ~ time	übergreifende Transferzeit
transient error	vorübergehender Fehler
transit call	Durchgangsverbindung, Transitverbindung
~ exchange	Transitvermittlung, Durchgangsvermittlungsstelle
broadband ~ exchange	Breitband-Transitvermittlung
~ node	Durchgangsknoten, Transitknoten, Zwischenknoten
~ traffic	Durchgangsverkehr, Transitverkehr
international ~ exchange	internationale Durchgangsvermittlungsstelle
transmission	Übertragung
~ and switching information	Nachrichenübermittlung (Nachrichtenübertragung + Nachrichtenverarbeitung)
~ link	Übertragungsstrecke
~ loss	Übertragungsdämpfung
~ path	Übertragungsweg, Fernmeldeweg
~ performance	Übertragungsleistung, Gesprächsgüte
~ power	Sendeleistung
~ quality	Übertragungsgüte, Übertragungsqualität
~ reliability	Übertragungssicherheit
~ section	Übermittlungsabschnitt
~ service	Übermittlungsdienst
analog ~	analoge Übertragung
asynchronous ~	asynchrone Übertragung
attempted ~	versuchte Übertragung
both-way ~	beidseitige Übertragung
digital ~	digitale Übertragung
envelope-mode ~	enveloperweise Übertragung
radio ~	drahtlose Übertragung
section-by-section ~	abschnittsweise Übertragung

serial ~	serielle Übertragung
simultaneous ~	simultane Übertragung
synchronous ~	synchrone Übertragung
two-way ~	beidseitige Übertragung
transmit vb	senden, übertragen
~ digitally	digital übertragen
~ vb a facsimile	Fernkopie, Faksimile übertragen
~ vb section by section	abschnittweise übertragen
transmit mode	Sendebetrieb
transmittal mode	Sendebetrieb
transmitter	Sender, Sendeeinrichtung
~ antenna	Sendeantenne
~ -receiver set	Sende-/Empfangseinrichtung
fixed ~	ortsfester Sender
mobile ~	Übertragungswagen
transmitting antenna	Sendeantenne
~ end	Sendeseite
transparent mode	Transparent-Modus
transponder	Transponder
transport layer	Transportschicht
transportable mobile station	tragbare Mobilstation, bewegliche Mobilstation
tree structure	Baumstruktur
trunk	Abnehmerleitung
~ circuit bothways	wechselseitiger Leitungssatz
~ exchange	Fernamt, Fernvermittlung
~ group	Anschlußgruppe, Leitungsbündel, Bündel
common ~ group	gemeinsames Leitungsbündel
testing ~ group	Prüfbündel
~ group splitting	Bündelspaltung, Bündeltrennung
~ line	Fernleitung, Fernverbindungsleitung
~ network	Fernleitungsnetz, Fernnetz
~ offering message	Aufschaltemeldung
~ type	Leitungsart
all ~s busy, ATB	alle Fernleitungen besetzt, äußere Blockierung

common serving ~	gemeinsame Abnehmerleitung
trunking	Bündelfunk, Kanalbündelung
~ arrangement	Gruppierung
tuning	Abgleich
turnkey system	schlüsselfertiges System
turnover (of customers/subscribers)	Fluktuationsrate
two-party line	Zweieranschluß
~ -way intercom system	Gegensprechanlage
~ -way splitting	Makeln bei der Abfragestelle
~ -way transmission	beidseitige Übertragung
~ -wire line	Zweidrahtleitung

U

umbrella cell	Schirmzelle
~ site	Großflächen-Funkstation
unabbreviated call number	Langrufnummer
unattended adj	unbedient, unbemannt, automatisch
~ exchange	unbemanntes Amt
~ reception (facsimile)	automatischer Empfang
unavailable time	nicht verfügbare Zeit
uncompleted call	nicht zustandegekommene Verbindung
~ call due to busy condition	wegen Besetztseins nicht zustandegekommene Verbindung
unconditional call forwarding ~	bedingungslos bedingungslose Anrufweiterleitung, unbedingte Anrufumlenkung
underlaid cell	unterlagerte Funkzone

undersea cable	Seekabel
undisturbed local operation	ungestörter Lokalbetrieb
unmanned	unbedient, unbemannt
~ exchange	unbemanntes Amt
unrestricted extension	voll amtsberechtigte Nebenstelle
unsuccessful call	erfolgloser Anruf
~ call attempt	erfolgloser Anrufversuch
unwanted emissions	unerwünschte Aussendungen
~ signal	ungewünschtes Signal
update vb	aktualisieren
updating request	Umbuchnachricht
upgradable adj	erweiterungsfähig
uplink (MS transmits, BS receives)	Aufwärtsstrecke
~ frequency	Aufwärtsfrequenz
upload vb	hochladen
upper half band	Oberband
upstream information	Rückinformationen
extraction of ~ information	Entnahme von Rückinformationen
urban areas	städtische Gebiete
usable field strength	Nutzfeldstärke
usage factor	Auslastungsgrad
~ pattern	Nutzungsverhalten
user	Teilnehmer, Anwender, Benutzer
~ class of service	Benutzerklasse, Teilnehmerbetriebsklasse
~ directory	Teilnehmerverzeichnis
~ equipment	Teilnehmergeräte, Teilnehmereinrichtungen
~ -friendly	benutzerfreundlich
~ friendliness	Benutzerfreundlichkeit
~ group	Benutzergruppe
closed ~ group	geschlossene Benutzergruppe
~ interface	Benutzerschnittstelle
~ -network interface	Teilnehmer-Netz-Schnittstelle

~ -network signalling	Benutzer-Netz-Signalisierung
~ part	Benutzerteil (ISDN)
~ -related sequence	teilnehmerbezogener Ablauf
~ signal channel	Nutzkanal
~ software	Anwendersoftware
switching ~ software	vermittlungstechnische Anwendersoftware
~ -to-user signalling, UUS	Teilnehmer-Teilnehmer-Zeichengabe
mobile ~	mobiler Teilnehmer
network ~ identifier	Teilnehmerkennung
stationary ~	stationärer Teilnehmer
utility trailer	Container

V

validation	Validierung
value-added network	Netz mit erweiterten Übertragungsmöglichkeiten
~ -added networks services, VANS	Netzdienstleistungen für Mehrwertdienste
~ -added services	Mehrwertdienste
vehicular mobile radio unit	Autotelefon
~ mobile station	fahrzeuggebundene Mobilstation
verified event	gesicherter Anreiz
vertex plate	Scheitelplatte (Antenne)
video communications	Bildkommunikation
video-conference	Videokonferenz, Bewegtbild-Telekonferenz
~ display telephone	Bildfernsprecher, Bildschirmtelefon
~ -phone	Bildfernsprecher
~ -phone conference	Bildkonferenz

~ -phoning	Bildfernsprechen
~ signal transmission	Bildsignalübertragung
full ~ teleconference	Bewegtbild-Telekonferenz
~ telephone	Bildschirmtelefon
~ -telephony	Bildfernsprechen
videotex	Bildschirmtext, Btx, Videotex
~ computer center	Btx-Zentrale
broadband ~	Breitband-Bildschirmtext
videotext	Videotext (für Empfang über Farbfernsehgerät)
virtual circuit	virtuelle Verbindung
visited exchange	besuchte Funkvermittlungsstelle
~ location register	Fremddatei
~ mobile services switching center, ~ MSC	besuchte Funkvermittlungsstelle
~ mobile services switching center area, ~ MSC area	Fremd-Bereich
~ network	besuchtes Netz
~ public land mobile network	besuchtes Mobilfunknetz
~ radio zone	Aufenthaltsfunkzone
visitor location register, VLR	Fremddatei, Besucherdatei
visual camp-on	optisches Anklopfen
~ signalling	optische Signalisierung
voice	Sprache
~ activity detection, VAD	Sprechaktivitätserkennung
~ and data network	Sprach- und Datennetz
~ and data switching	Sprach- und Datenvermittlung
~ band	Sprachband (Frequenzen)
~ channel	Sprechkanal
~ /data PBX	Sprach- und Daten-Nebenstellenanlage
~ -frequency range	Sprachfrequenzbereich
~ -frequency (VF) signalling	Tonfrequenzwahl, Tonwahl
~ mailbox	Sprachspeicherdienst, Sprachbox
~ mail service	Sprachspeicherdienst
~ message	Durchsage
~ network	Sprachnetz

~ prompting	akustische Bedienerführung
~ quality	Sprachqualität
enhanced ~ quality	erhöhte Sprachqualität
high ~ quality	hohe Sprachqualität
~ service	Sprachdienst
~ signal	Sprachsignal, Sprechsignal
~ -store-and-forward service	Sprachspeicherdienst
~ terminal	Sprachterminal
~ transmission	Sprachübertragung
voltage-sensitive adj	spannungsempfindlich
V-series interfaces	V-Serie-Schnittstellen
V-24-interface	V-24-Schnittstelle

W

waiting call	wartende Belegung
~ queue	Warteschlange
wait vb to be answered (call)	anstehen
~ to be attended (subscriber)	anstehen
~ to be served (service request)	anstehen
WAN (wide area network)	großflächiges Kommunikationsnetz
wanted signal	gewünschtes Signal
waveguide	Hohlleiter, Wellenleiter
semirigid ~	biegbarer Hohlleiter
wave length multiplexer	Wellenlängenmultiplexer
~ propagation	Wellenausbreitung
weight vb	bewerten, gewichten
whip antenna	Peitschenantenne

"who are you" key   Abfragetaste

wide area network, WAN   großflächiges Kommunikationsnetz

wideband (see also broadband)   Breitband
~ communications   Breitbandkommunikation
~ integrated fiber optical   breitbandiges integriertes Glas-
  long-distance communica-   faser-Fernmeldenetz (BIGFERN)
  tions network
~ LAN (local area ~ net-   lokales Breitbandnetz
  work)
~ optical fiber local com-   breitbandiges integriertes Glas-
  munications network   faser-Fernmelde-Ortsnetz (BIGFON)
~ service   Breitbanddienst
~ transmission   Breitbandübertragung

wire   Draht, Ader (Kabel)
~ connection   drahtgebundene Übertragung
~ less   drahtlos
~ less PABX   schnurlose Nebenstellenanlage
~ line network   Drahtnetz
~ tapping   Anzapfen

word error rate   Wortfehlerquote

work vb in synchronism   synchron arbeiten

working/standby mode   Aktiv-/Reserve-Betriebsart

World Administrative Radio   Weltfunkverwaltungskonferenz,
  Conference, WARC   weltweite Funkverwaltungskonferenz
~ Administrative Radio   weltweite Funkverwaltungskonferenz
  Conference for Mobile   für Mobilfunk
  Services, WARC-MOB
~ Administrative Radio   weltweite Funkverwaltungskonferenz
  Conference for Orbital   für Satelliten-Dienste
  Services, WARC-ORB

worldwide communications net-   Weltkommunikationsnetz
  work
~ pay phone   Weltmünzer, Weltmünzfernsprecher
~ switched data network   Weltdatenwählnetz

wrist-watch pager   Armbanduhr-Funkrufempfänger

wrong number   falsch verbunden

X

X.25 protocol	X.25-Protokoll
X-series interfaces	y-Serie-Schnittstellen
x/y interface	x/y-Schnittstelle

Z

zero-loss circuit	verlustlose Leitung
zone	Zone
~ of silence	tote Zone
~ rate	Zonengebühr
radio ~	Funkzone
silent ~	tote Zone
zoning	Verzonung

Neue Möglichkeiten für den Betriebsfunk

Bündelfunk ist der Ausweg aus dem Dilemma überlasteter Kanäle im Bereich des Betriebsfunks. Wenn Sie über die Neuanschaffung einer Betriebsfunkanlage nachdenken und sich über Netze, Betreiber, Geräte und Kosten informieren möchten, dann ist dieses Buch genau das richtige. Anhand der in Deutschland bereits installierten und geplanten Netze wird gezeigt, wie komfortabel Bündelfunk arbeitet.

Bündelfunk in Deutschland
Neue Wege für die betriebliche Kommunikation.
(Pernsteiner) 2. Aufl. 1992. 190 Seiten,
98 Abbildungen, 12 Tabellen, kartoniert,
DM 29,80
ISBN 3-7723-**4461-5**

Von der analogen zur digitalen Modulation

Der Einzug der digitalen Nachrichtenübertragung ist nicht mehr aufzuhalten, da diese leistungsfähiger und störsicherer ist. Die verwendeten Verfahren der Quadraturmodulation sind noch weitgehend unbekannt. Dieses Buch stellt, ausgehend von den analogen Modulationsarten, den Übergang zu den entsprechenden digitalen Verfahren her, ohne sich in mathematischen Betrachtungen zu verlieren.

Einstieg in die digitalen Modulationsverfahren
Grundlagen, Anwendungen und Meßtechnik.
(Sonnde/Hoeckstein) 1992. 171 Seiten,
127 Abbildungen, kartoniert, **DM 49,–**
ISBN 3-7723-**5872-1**

Franzis-Fachbücher erhalten Sie in jeder Buch- und Fachhandlung.
Preisänderungen vorbehalten.

Franzis'
Franzis-Verlag GmbH & Co. KG., Buchvertrieb, Karlstraße 35
8000 München 2, Telefon 0 89/51 17-2 85, **Tag-und-Nacht-Service: Telefax 0 89/51 17-3 77**